THE APOCALYPSE HAS BEGUN

A View of the Restoration of the World for the Second Coming of Christ

LOUIS A. KELSCH

THE APOCALYPSE HAS BEGUN
A VIEW OF THE RESTORATION OF THE WORLD
FOR THE SECOND COMING OF CHRIST.

iUniverse books may be ordered through booksellers or by contacting:

iUniverse
1663 Liberty Drive
Bloomington, IN 47403
www.iuniverse.com
1-800-Authors (1-800-288-4677)

ISBN: 978-1-4759-9910-5 (sc)
ISBN: 978-1-4759-9911-2 (hc)
ISBN: 978-1-4759-9912-9 (e)

Library of Congress Control Number: 2013912652

Print information available on the last page.

iUniverse rev. date: 03/13/2015

CONTENTS

AUTHORS PREFACE

This book discusses events of the last days. Not the second coming, but the events that lead up to the second coming of the Lord Jesus Christ. The events that prepare the earth, to make it worthy and clean for His presence to abide here.

I am a Mormon and have been all my life. I love the Church of Jesus Christ of Latter Day Saints. And I have learned that the LDS Church today, doctrinally and organizationally, looks exactly like the Church that Christ organized in the meridian of time. This Church was founded on the principle of revelation from God and is not a Protestant Church. We did not come out of the Catholic Church either by protesting the teaching of that Church or by the process of excommunication from that Church.

We are, truly, an original American Church.

The founding Prophet of the LDS Church, Joseph Smith, wrote "Articles of Faith" in March 1842. This writing represents thirteen statements made by the Prophet that summarizes some of the basic doctrine of the Church and are also considered scripture. These "Articles of Faith" are basic teachings for all members of the Church. These teachings start at ages 3-11 for our primary children. In fact as a rite-of-passage into the teenage classes a primary child will be asked to recite, from memory, several of these articles and explain their meanings. The tenth article of faith reads as follows: *"We believe in the literal gathering of Israel and in the restoration of the Ten Tribes; that Zion will be built upon the American continent; that Christ will reign personally upon the earth; and, that the earth will be renewed and receive its paradisiacal glory".*

This scripture speaks to a time when the earth will be renewed, to its original configuration, and will receive its paradisiacal glory.

Several of the paradisiacal conditions will be the personal presence of the Lord Jesus Christ, the absence of sin and the restoration of the earth to its Edenic configuration and appearance. A true utopia.

This book is my view of the Last Days and how, I believe that the events spoken of in this tenth article of faith will come to past.

These writings are offered as an incentive to repent and turn to the Lord with full purpose of heart.

Based on LDS scripture I, and my family and my many LDS friends, will be physically impacted by the "Last Days" before anyone else in the world.

Most of my friends in the Church are very well informed about what will happen in these "last Days" and are looking forward to it.

We study these days . . . we look forward to these days, . . . we sing of these days and we pray for these days to come.

We live in the dispensation that all prophets for the last six millennia have spoken of or prophesied about. Indeed we are living in the most talked about dispensation in the history of the world.

And since the Lord has seen fit to make this time of earth our time to be here it is apparent He wants us to have these experiences and to be participants as well.

And also since the Lord has placed us here at this time I know that He has no intention of permitting us to be ignorant on this subject or any other gospel subject. To the contrary, I am certain that, every sincere and prayerful effort to understand future events will be rewarded.

Also, I think I am safe in saying that the subject, of the "last days" has a very high fascination threshold among all "Christians". Everyone seems to be concerned about the "Apocalypse" and with very good reason . . . we are an evil society and we know it.

My thoughts were continually filled with questions of when and how? Was there an order in prophesied events? What was going to happen to me and my family and to our Christian colleagues?

There is really only one proper way to review and try to understand this subject and that is through the influence of the Holy Ghost such as promised in John 16:13.

I have made no attempt to analyze all revealed scripture on the subject of the cleansing of the earth of all wickedness. That would be a very large undertaking as virtually all prophets of all dispensations have spoken of events pertaining to this last dispensation of time.

Then too I was curious to know who the Lord intends to save from this cleansing process and why?

One of the foremost questions in my mind was . . . when? When were these things going to happen?

And that question has been answered to my satisfaction.

Once again I have not written about the Second Coming, I have written about the preparation of the earth, . . . for the Second Coming. If the angels in Heaven don't know the time of the Second Coming its most certain, . . . I don't either (See Doctrine & Covenants (D/C) 49:7).

Time is short and I firmly believe that all of my children and grand children will live to see this earth cleansed, and transformed into a terrestrial (millennial) or paradisiacal estate.

I believe that there are some trying times ahead for the Latter Day Saints, and that our faith will be sorely tested. I also believe that such trials will not be more than we can bear, and that is a very important point to remember. And that just as there are trials ahead for us, I also know that there are times ahead . . . of joy unspeakable, and spiritual experiences unlike anything we have ever known, or imagined.

A very sad time will come when the Lord will separate out of His church, *"the foolish virgins from the wise"* (see D/C 63:54).

In fact, our prophets have told us that the beginning of the terrible events of the last days will begin on the Lords Church. In the Doctrine & Covenants (D/C) we read, *"And upon my house shall it begin, and from my house shall it go forth, saith the Lord"* (D/C 112:25).

The Lord is no hypocrite. It appears He will cleanse His Church before He cleanses the world. And by this will all men know which church is the only true Church on earth, if they have the *"eyes to see and the ears to hear"*. However if He will show a strong hand with His own Church, and with "foolish virgins", what will He do with the world? As Peter declared,

"And if the righteous scarcely be saved where shall the ungodly and sinner appear" (1 Peter 4:18)?

These writings represent my beliefs and testimony and I am solely responsible for the thoughts expressed and the manner in which quotations were used. If there are any imperfections in this book they are mine and mine alone.

The scriptures referenced are taken from the books as follows:

King James Version (KJV) of the Holy Bible, the old and new testament.

Book of Mormon (B of M or B/M), a compilation of revelations to the early inhabitants of the American continents.

Doctrine and Covenants (D/C) a compliation of revelations to LDS Prophets.

Pearl of Great Price, (P of GP), or references to the books of Moses and Abraham. Revelations that describe the spiritual and physical creation of the earth and other unique events.

CHAPTER 1

INTRODUCTION

I n this writing I speak to my family, friends, associates and fellow latter-day-saints and those thoughtful Christian colleagues, who bring pamphlets to my door.

Chapters 2-5 review scriptures that specifically apply to the "Last Days". This review illustrate events that will one day, impact the entire world. These chapters are an evaluation of existing scripture and review the methods the Lord will use to neutralize Satan and prepare the earth for the Lords millennial reign.

All of the circumstances illustrated in chapters 2-5 speak of dire and terrible things that will befall man, in the . . . last days. Events that will virtually kill many, many people who refuse to humble themselves and repent of their sins and change their life.

Chapters 6 through 14 were written, originally as white papers, for my library and my family and also shared with a number of close friends. Later the thought come . . . why not form these papers into a book?

Chapter 7, "Warning", is somewhat unique as it is a brief summary of last day events and associated timing, written to the world at large over the issue of the Mayan calendar. In fact an effort was made to publish this "Warning" to local communities through several newspapers.

The devastation described in these chapters is unprecedented in the history of the world. I believe the apocalypse will very literally isolate all people from communities, and local and Federal government . . . even from Churches. These horrific events will force us to recognize that there is indeed a God and He is not pleased with us.

I am certain . . . the Lord takes no delight in these prophesied devastations. Peter the Chief Apostle, a man who walked and talked with the Lord, and knew Him personally writes in 2 Peter 3:8-9, *"The Lord is not slack concerning His promise, as some count slackness; but is longsuffering to us-ward, not willing that any should parish, but that all should come to repentance"*.

The key thought here is repentance. If we don't repent we cannot qualify for the Lords atonement.

The remainder of this introduction is divided into four sections; Pre-Apocalyptic Events, The Apocalyptic Events, Contemporary Tribulation and Summary.

Pre-Apocalyptic Events

Preparation of the Elect

The Lord has told the LDS Church in a number of different ways and places how to meet the standard of excellence that He has set as criteria for exaltation in His kingdom. For example in the parable of the ten virgins in Matt 25:1-12, the Lord illustrates very clearly what His expectations are to meet His standard of excellence. This parable likens His Church to 10 virgins. Five of these virgins were not adequately prepared to enter into the marriage and were rejected, and labeled as foolish, because they were unprepared and had ignored counsel to be prepared.

And again, in Luke 17:5-10, the Apostles ask the Lord . . . *"Lord increase our faith"*. And then He tells them a parable, of a servant working in the field for his master. And at the end of the day the servant comes in from the field, and does the master say sit down and have something to eat? No! The Lord replies. The master says to the servant, first fix my dinner, then fix one for yourself. Does the master then thank the servant for all that he has done, and the Lord answered . . . no! Because the servant has only done his duty . . . he is still an unprofitable servant. What then is a profitable servant . . . one may ask? And I answer. One who takes the initiative to add to the build-up and growth of the kingdom on both sides of the veil.

In modern revelation the Lord provides clear insight into His expectations of a servant. In D/C 58:26-29, the Lord declares that it is not right that He must command in all things, and that he who must be commanded in all things is a slothful servant. The Lord then explains that men should be <u>anxiously engaged</u>, in a good cause, and bring to pass many good things of their own free will, because the power is in them to do that, because of their agency. The Lord gave us agency and a reasoning intellect, and He does not expect to have to lead us around as children. The Lord then explains that anyone who does nothing until he is commanded, and receives that commandment with a doubtful heart, and keeps the commandment slothfully, the same is damned. Notwithstanding that person is a virgin. In this scripture the guiding thought is *"where much is given, much is expected"*. These foregoing paragraphs illustrate the Lords expectations of His Saints in these last days.

The Apocalyptic Events

3ʳᵈ Nephi 21 of the book of Mormon

This chapter summarizes 3rd Nephi 21:13-29, which occurred about 34 AD. I find it interesting that Micah, in Micah 5:8-14, a prophet of the Old Testament who ministered about 721 BC, speaks to the identical prophesies of verses 14-18 of 3ʳᵈ Nephi 21. These scriptures are basically a warning to the gentiles, of the last days, to repent. And also a strong warning is issued to the remnants of the house of Israel who also refuse to repent and join the Church.

These scriptures prophesy that the sons of Jacob, in the last days, are going to go forth among the gentiles as a young Lion among sheep that will kill and tear with impunity and nothing will stop them. Such destruction by the "Sons of Jacob", is not without precedence.

Just exactly who these sons of Jacob are, other than of the house of Israel, is plainly discussed in the following writing.

Now who are the "remnants" of the house of Israel, and who are the "Gentiles"?

Background

But first a little explanation. The Lord in ancient days made great covenants or promises to Abraham, the great Patriarch, his son Isaac and his grandson Jacob (Israel)

A summary of these covenants are as follows:

4

Covenant of Salvation, . . . Baptism

Covenant of exaltation . . . To receive the
Melchizedek Priesthood and Celestial Marriage
and eternal increase.

Covenant that Christ would come through his
lineage.

Covenants of possession of certain choice lands for
eternity.

Covenant of an enormous posterity.

Covenant that all of these covenants would be
offered to his mortal posterity.

(See Mormon Doctrine, pg. 13, by Bruce R
McConkie).

These covenants are recited here to illustrate just how much the Lord loved these three Patriarchs. And the "Restoration" demonstrates how zealous the Lord is in fulfilling these covenants to the descendants of these Patriarchs.

These same covenants were made with Abraham's son Isaac, and his grandson Jacob. The Lord later named Jacob, . . . Israel. It is Israel's descendants we will be talking about.

These three men, Abraham, Isaac and Jacob (Israel) known as the Patriarchs, were exceedingly valiant, in the service of the Lord, during their lifetime. The Lord loved them and covenanted to bless them that through their descendants the whole world would be blessed by the Melchizedek Priesthood that was to continue in their lineage. Also their descendants would be as numerous as the sands of the seashore.

Abraham had many descendants of whom came many nations who are called Hebrews.

But when the scriptures refer to the descendants of Israel, the remnant of Israel, or the Israelites, they are referring to the descendants of Jacob or Israel, the Grandson of Abraham. The term "gentile" also has several meanings. One meaning is that the one so designated has no blood of Israel flowing in his veins. Another meaning is a spiritual connotation unique to the LDS Church and has reference to any individual who has not received or who has rejected the teachings of the LDS Church and the call to faith and repentance.

The house of Israel are the descendants of the great patriarch Israel. Israel had 12 sons, by four wives of whom came great nations. All who are not of this lineage are gentiles. For example the Jews who are now residing in Judea are of the tribe of Judah, one of the 12 sons of Israel, and represent one-twelfth of the house of Israel, the other eleven tribes having been dispersed through out the world to *"the corners of the earth"* because of wickedness.

This is a very sad comment on the tribes of Israel, because the Lord gave them great promises if they would but remain faithful to Him. For example in Deuteronomy 28:1 We read, *"And it shall come to pass, if thou shalt harken diligently unto the voice of the Lord thy God, to observe and to do all His commandments which I command thee this day, that the Lord thy God will set thee on high above all nations of the earth"*. It would seem that if ancient Israel had been faithful they would have ruled the world instead of being dispersed through-out the world because of wickedness.

The scriptures in this writing deal with the "Sons of Jacob", or descendants of the house of Israel, and the wicked gentiles of the last days.

Sons of Jacob

This chapter will review specific scriptures where the role of the 'Sons of Jacob" is prophesied.

The only reason the Lord would send forth such a destructive power, as the role these "sons of Jacob" are to play, is to destroy wickedness.

What I have observed through the scriptures is the great efforts made by the Lord to bring the people of the world to repentance.

The devastation that may be wrought by the "Sons of Jacob", is not without precedent in the scriptures.

For example when the Israelites were delivered out of 400 years of slavery to the Egyptian Pharaohs, and taken into the wildness by Moses, they were eventually led to the promised land, where each of the 12 tribes were promised, by the Lord, that they were to receive an inheritance in this "promised land". However this promised land was already occupied by nations of other peoples. By the Amorites, Bashan, seven nations of Canaanites, Hittites, Perizzites, Hivites, Jebusites, Amalekites, Moabites, great city of Jericho, Philistines, and the Anakims (remnant of the giants).

The Lord told Moses and later Joshua to destroy most of these people, *"by the edge of the sword"*, and the Israelites were to take possession of their houses and lands; their fields and crops that were still in the fields ready to be harvested. This was the land *"flowing with milk and honey"*, that the Lord promised the descendants of Israel.

But why would the Lord decree destruction of these nations at the hands of Israel?

Because they were idol worshippers, and practiced sexual perversion, and the Lord considered them to be so evil, they were worthy of destruction. They practiced the same sins as Sodom and Gomorrah, plain cities that were destroyed by fire rained down from the skies, in Abraham's day.

Today we as a global society are guilty of the very same sins. And the general attitude of the present day world populace is that God will merely "wink" at our sins and life will go on as usual. But God has made His position very clear, "He is no respecter of persons". Our society may very well get the same treatment as those nations that were in the way of the tribes of Israel several thousand years ago. And why not, we are every bit as evil as they were. So as He did anciently, through the tribes of Israel, the Lord may cry repentance to the gentiles through the "Sons of Jacob", at some time in the future.

Book of Revelations 8-11

This chapter is taken from the book of Revelations. A book that was written by John the apostle while he was exiled to the penal colony on the isle of Patmos. Chapters 1-3 of the book of revelations are addressed to the Seven Churches of that day, and chapters 4-22 are revelations that are as yet futuristic, and deal with the Lords victory over evil and the restoration of all things. My review will consider verses in chapters 8-11, relating to seven plagues that are designed by the Deity to do three things: First, call the wicked to repentance. Second, cleanse the world of those who refuse to repent. Third, herald the day when the Lord has victory over evil. These "Last Days" revelations are unique among scriptures in that they quantify the amount of destruction to be accomplished, as a result of these plagues, and provide a time when these cataclysmic events will begin and how long many of them will last.

Doctrine and Covenants, section 29

This chapter is taken from a revelation that was given to the Prophet Joseph Smith in Sept 1830 in the presence of six Elders of the Church, prior to a Church conference. In this revelation the Lord declares that a *"a decree hath gone forth from the Father that they (the elect) shall be gathered in unto one place"*. A decree is a divine mandate. This is an unequivocal declaration by the Lord that there is to be a gathering of the "elect". And the purpose for the gathering of the elect is *"to prepare their hearts and be prepared in all things against the day when tribulation and desolation are sent forth upon the wicked"*. (See verse 8). Where is the gathering to occur and who are the elect? As to where the gathering will occur, I refer you to History of the Church, Vol. ll., Page 254, where the Prophet Joseph Smith explains that this gathering is to be; to that place known as Jackson County, Missouri, and the place is to be called Zion, or the New Jerusalem. The elect are those who have been baptized, kept the commandments, received the Priesthood (for the men), gone through the temple, and been sealed, and who endure to the end (See Mormon Doctrine, by Bruce R. McConkie, page 217-218).

Contemporary Tribulation

Present day warnings from Deity

Even today, as I write, in the state of Arkansas, and Oklahoma, great rain has fallen resulting in flooding and even deaths. The rains were noted by the national weather bureau to be greater than the 500-year level.

We have had, just recently, in the year 2010 devastating earthquakes in Haiti, and Chile, that took the lives of thousands and destroyed the homes of hundreds of thousands.

Pakistan, in the region known as SWAT has experienced unprecedented rain that has left an estimated 20,000,000 people homeless and in misery from flooding. Myself and many fellow Christians believe that these events are all calls to repent. Wars that are on going are also calls to repentance. If people would repent and come to the Lord with full purpose of heart is it not reasonable, to believe, that these things would cease to be?

Why do we not learn from the past? Through out the history of men the Prophets have made it clear how God displays His disappointment with man. On one occasion He was so upset with man that he removed them all from the earth by a flood accept for Noah and his family who he deemed righteous enough to save. Why does man prefer to think of such devastation as folklore rather than learn Gods inclinations and the point at which His tolerance level has been reached? Its all their in black and white if we but read it and accept it.

Accepting the writings of ancient prophets is easy when one realizes that God is omnipotent. If He is truly omnipotent then the scriptures we have today, all of them, are what He wants us to have and are adequate for guidance and salvation as written. If someone feels that ancient scriptures are folklore, then their God is not omnipotent. They needn't fear Him or for that matter look to Him for succor.

The earth ripens in iniquity

Today hatred is strong in the world. The Arabs hate the Jews, and strangely enough they seem to hate each other as well, because there is constant reports of war and killings between the Sunnis and the Shiites, who are differing philosophies within the Arab, . . . Muslim faith.

In Europe the Bosnians and the Serbs hate each other. The leaders of North Korea hate everyone, especially South Korea. Islam, the descendants of Ishmael want to rule the world and force everyone to believe as they do or die. Pakistan and India, both nuclear powers, are constantly on the brink of war.

The Irish, for years, have experienced hatred between there Catholic and Protestant citizens resulting in suburban wars and killings. The USA, and associated military coalition, is at war with the Taliban in the nation of Afghanistan. And at present most nations hate, fear or envy, the USA.

Within our own nation hate is strong between those who love government under the constitution, and those who want to abolish the constitution an instrument, ordained by God through our founding Fathers, that has made us the mightiest nation on earth. In fact the Marxist policies of our current President and his administration is dividing the nation.

The family is under attack

Families are so dysfunctional, in all levels of our society, that street gangs who offer a support base for neglected youth are prolific. And, being well organized, engage in stealing and murder, and the killing off of competitors, etc. It has been reported that a gang initiation requirement is to commit a murder. No one in particular, just any random killing will do.

The method of choice to full fill this murderous and insane initiation is called a drive-by-shooting.

Homosexuals are always in the news. Demanding the passage of laws that favor their sexual orientation such as legalizing their marriages or civil unions, to obtain advantages under tax laws. They even want their life style taught in schools.

Our society is conspicuous, in that, the unprincipled people and the indifferent ones out number the conscientious and the principled people. A sad condition that flies in the face of Gods expectations for His children. One could say that evil is rampant in our world. We too are ripe with iniquity.

Cleansing of the earth

The Lord will cry repentance to us through natural disasters at first. These disasters will be unlike anything ever experienced. The destruction of plant life, the poisoning of water, earthquakes and volcanoes, and great hailstorms. These events in and of them selves may take a great toll of life, but should motivate some to repent.

The events that will follow, the initial wave of destruction, are more destructive than any previously experienced and are referred to as the "worst woes that are yet to come". These "worst woes" are warfare whose purpose is to depopulate.

However, their will be those "who will not take up a weapon against his neighbor". They will have to flee to Zion for safety.

I don't know where the principle area of warfare will start however, I believe, much of it will involve the areas around Jerusalem, and eventually Jerusalem itself, where 200,000,000 will wage war (See Rev 9:16). And the North and South Americas, and the isles of the sea, where the "sons of Jacob" may prevail, in their task of death and destruction.

This warfare will be followed by a cleansing of the earth by fire. The Church of the Devil will be consumed by fire. Those who continue to espouse the error of the day, and forego repentance will all parish, by fire.

By the end only those who are qualified as the elect of God, and those who flee to Zion for safety, and those who the Lord will "gather", for His own purposes, . . . will be spared.

What is wickedness

Something needs to be said about the term "wicked". This word is used a great deal in the scriptures that pertain to "The Last Days", and its important to know what it means.

There is of course gross wickedness, such as murder, adultery and fornication, homosexuality, sodomy, pornography, idolatry, stealing, cheating, lying, malicious gossip, blasphemers, obscenities, vulgarity, profanity, pride and those who feel that "the ends justifies the means". These are sins of commission.

Then there is the wickedness of indifference. Of not following the counsel of the Lord. Of preferring to remain independent of the commitments and the sacrifices that the Lord asks of us.

Then there is the wickedness of doing what the Lord asks but . . . grudgingly and avoiding commitments that require some sacrifice and take "too much of ones time".

The only acceptable accomplishment to the lord is to qualify to come home to the presence of Heavenly Father.

All else that falls short of that supernal goal, is to a lesser or greater extent, . . . wickedness.

Summary

The terrifying and frightening events discussed in the following chapters, briefly reviewed above, describe the Lords victory over evil, as it pertains to this earth. These dire predictions are also a message from the Lord, encouraging all mortals to repent.

If all mortals were indeed to fully repent and turn to the Lord; Satan would be bound, by the rejection of all he represents, and the earth would be translated as was the city of Enoch and the great community known as the "city of Salem", ruled by the great high Priest, . . . Melchizedek. But alas it seems that we mortals only learn the hard way. There is no doubt in my mind that the prophecies briefly referred to above will come to pass.

As I have reviewed these apocalyptic predictions I have noted that the inclination of the Lord is to meter out His cleansing, or call to repentance. For example, it appears that, He will first send disasters of nature, that pertain to natural phenomenon. Such as the sun being darkened and moon appearing as blood. Earthquakes, terrible storms, famine, erupting volcanoes and etc. These are warnings.

Those who are the honorable and more principled people of the world will flee to Zion for safety.

Finally when all is done and the earth is cleansed of wickedness, and the unrepentant, . . . then, I believe that, the Lord will appear and initiate the millennial period of the earth. And those who remain and have repented and qualified to remain with this world will enjoy a fullness of the presence of the Lord. And in those days the knowledge of the Lord will cover the earth like a flood.

CHAPTER 2

3ᴿᴰ NEPHI 21:13-29

This scripture in the Book of Mormon was written about 34 AD, and is addressed to the gentiles of the America's, who would be established as a free people. If they believe and repent they will be saved. If they do not they shall be cut off and destroyed. In the last days one of the methods the Lord will use to call the world to repentance or destroy the wicked, if they reject, Him is described below.

13. The remnant of the sons of Jacob, will be as a young lion among the sheep and shall destroy all of their enemies.
   (See writing entitled "Sons of Jacob", for a brief analysis on who these Sons of Jacob may be, and who their enemies are.)

14. In that day the Lord will cut off the horses and chariots of the wicked, gentiles.
   (This may have reference to removing from the gentiles any escape mechanisms, from the terrible destructive force of the "terrible sons of Jacob". (See also Micah 5:10). To the prophet 3ʳᵈ Nephi horses and chariots in prophetic vision would be cars, and he sees that they are rendered useless. Perhaps because of the events described in the next verse).

15. **The Lord will cut off all the cities and strongholds of the gentiles.**

(The streets of the cities will be broken up, and the cities become desolate. (See 1 Nephi 14:21. See also Micah 5:11). With broken up city streets flight by automobile will be impossible, the wicked gentiles will be captive within their own cities and strongholds. Apparently the initial damage caused by the beginning of the apocalypse will have rendered the streets useless for automobiles).

16. **The Lord will cut off all witchcraft's and soothsayers.**

(This has to do with Satan worship, or doing the bidding of Satan. A soothsayer is Satan's substitute for a Prophet or Seer. These practices were common among the kings and nations the ancient Israelites were commanded to destroy. The Lord will show no more compassion to modern man who practice these abominations than He did to those who did so anciently. See Mormon doctrine, "soothsayer". See also Micah 5:12).

17. **The Lord will cut off graven images and standing images of the gentiles.**

(These are things made by the hand of man that are more precious to the possessor than God. (See also Micah 5:13). The things the gentiles will worship are money, power, the honor and adoration of man, material possessions, and objects of lust, and self-gratification).

18. **The Lord will pluck up the groves, and destroy the cities.**

(The term "groves" anciently was a living tree or tree like pole, set up as an object of worship, being symbolic of the female or productive principle in nature. And is associated with idolatry and immorality, and for this reason was rejected by the Prophets of Israel. See also Micah 5:14, and bible dictionary page 697. That which is comparable to "groves" that exists in our society today could be the entire "Sex Industry" in the world. Also the cities are to be destroyed).

19. **The Lord will do away with all lying, deceiving, envying, strife's, priest-crafts, and whoredoms.**

(Priest-craft is Satan's answer to the Priesthood. They are people who preach for hire, who teach doctrine of man mingled with scripture. There are three ways to do away with whoredoms. Either the people involved repent and control their passions, or make their intimacy legal in the eyes of the Lord or they are destroyed).

20. At that day the Lord will cut off all from among His people, who are of the house of Israel, who do not repent.

(I believe that the term "His people" has reference to His Church. I believe that those who will be cut off are they who are "casual" in their faithfulness, and also, this statement could have reference to those who are descendants of Jacob, either by adoption or blood lineage, who reject the missionaries of the Church. These will all be cut off if they do not repent.)

21. Referring to those described in verse 20; the Lord will execute vengeance and fury upon them, as upon the heathen, such as they have not heard.

(For generations the Lord has, time after time, given the Israelites the opportunity to repent and to return to Him. Those in this dispensation who remain unrepentant after the Lord shows His strong hand will find no mercy from a rebuffed God. This is also applicable to members of the LDS Church who are casual, and careless in their stewardship. They are the foolish 5 Virgins and will be rejected. These people have all received personal witnesses from the Lord . . . and have testimonies. And because of their testimonies have joined the Church. But they have chosen not to be valiant in the testimony of Jesus. Where much is given, . . . much is expected. He will treat them the same as the heathen, with punishment that exceeds anything known to man).

22-23. But if these people (referring to those of verse 20) will repent and join the Church, and be numbered among the remnant of Jacob, they will participate in building the New Jerusalem.

(In this scripture we are told that those referred to in verse 20 who are brought into the depths of humility by tribulation and repent will be spared and will have the job and the privilege of doing brick and mortar work in the New Jerusalem).

24. And the people referred to in verse 20, who repent, shall assist in the gathering of the Lords people into the New Jerusalem.

(The Lords people are gathered to Independence, Missouri where a city and Temple will be built and the city will be called, "New Jerusalem". The people referred to in verse 20, who repent, are to assist in this gathering. They will work under the direction of the tribe of Ephraim. Ephraim is the tribe of leadership and holds the keys of the Priesthood).

25. And the Lord will come down in there midst.

(There is to be a great Priesthood gathering at Adam-Ondi-Ahmen, in the state of Missouri, in the area known as Far West, Missouri. And the Lord will appear and receive the Priesthood keys from Father Adam, who will have first received dispensational keys from every Prophet down to the latest Prophet in this dispensation of time. I believe that this great priesthood meeting, and the return of all keys to the Lord, will occur just prior to the Lords Second Coming and after the saints are established in the New Jerusalem).

26. And then shall the work of the Father commence among the dispersed, even the lost tribes of Israel.

(The lost tribes are to come out of the North and come to Zion to receive their blessings at the hands of Ephraim. The tribes of Judah and their associates will return to old Jerusalem and the descendants of Joseph will return to the Americas and the New Jerusalem (see D/C commentary by Hyrum Smith & Janne Sjodahl page 726 and D/C 110:11).

27. Then the work shall commence among all the dispersed that they may call upon the Lord.

(All the dispersed remnants of Israel who will flee to Zion will be gathered and will be taught the gospel that they may learn to call upon the Lord. The Lord is zealous in fulfilling the covenants He made to their progenitor Israel (Jacob).

28 Then shall the work commence among all people to gather them home to the land of their inheritance.

(The descendants of Israel who qualify and are saved will eventually gather in Jerusalem (Judea). Where as the worthy descendants of Joseph, will gather in the New Jerusalem (Missouri). These two Jerusalem's are the centers of the lands of inheritance).

29. And they shall go out from all nations, not in haste, nor by flight, and will have the protection of the Father.

(The gathering of the elect or any who are permitted to flee to Zion, in the last days, is to be presided over by the Lord. They will not go in haste, nor be driven out, nor have to flee for their lives. It will be an orderly exodus under divine protection. The scriptural inference that they will have the protection of the Father indicates that circumstances, relative to any who are "gathered", may be hazardous, and require divine protection).

CHAPTER 3

SONS OF JACOB

This writing speaks to four scriptures. Three from the book of Mormon; 3 Nephi 20:16, 3 Nephi 21:12 and Mormon 5:24 and one from the Old Testament; Micah 5:8. These referenced scriptures are almost identical to those referenced in chapter 2, however there is a surprising alteration in prophesy that is worthy of review.

These scriptures all have the same thing in common. They speak of a segment of the descendants of Israel, known as the "Sons of Jacob", who in the last days may play a frightening and terrible role of destruction. Their role of destruction is described as that of a young lion among sheep. A young lion kills for the excitement of the moment, and his devastation is total. These prophecies describe circumstances that would be so horrific and powerful that there will be nothing to stop the slaughter and no mercy will be shown or even considered, unless the wicked repent.

In these scriptures the Lord introduced an alternative thought relative to certain destruction causing these scriptures to differ from those of chapter 2.

<u>3 Nephi 20:16</u> Then shall a remnant of the house of Jacob, be in the midst of the gentiles, like a lion among the flocks of sheep, **who if he goeth through** and treadeth down and teareth in pieces, and none can deliver.

(A terrible demise to be experienced by the gentiles if they do not repent. The victims of this great destruction are hard core unrepentant. Many natural disasters will occur, to motivate people to repent before the killing of individuals will happen. By the time the Lord has cried repentance to the wicked through natural calamity and disaster, many will be motivated to repent and those that are left are the hardcore wicked. The underlined phrase, "if he goeth through" I believe, puts the event on hold pending divine authorization).

<u>Micah 5:8</u> Says the same thing, as 3 Nephi 20:16 as it pertains to the Sons of Jacob, and what they will do in the last days. However here again the phrase **"if he goeth through"** is present. In my mind this says that the Lord may or may not permit the Sons of Jacob to destroy like a lion among sheep, depending on the wickedness of the people, after the initial days of tribulation.

<u>3 Nephi, 21:12</u> And my people who are a remnant of Jacob shall be among the Gentiles as a young lion among flocks of sheep, **and if he goeth through** both treadeth down and teareth to pieces and none can deliver.

(If the gentiles do not repent, the sons of Jacob may be permitted to kill as wantonly and with as little compassion as a young lion among helpless sheep, and no one will be able to deliver them from this terrible destruction. The phrase "and none can deliver" causes me to feel that the gentiles will be incapable of defending themselves).

<u>Mormon 5:24</u> Therefore repent ye and humble yourselves before Him, **lest a remnant of the seed of Jacob** go among you as a lion and tear you in pieces, and there is none to deliver.
(Again a divine warning to the gentiles of the last days and an invitation to repent. The term "lest" indicates to my mind that the Lord may not permit this destruction

to occur. I believe it depends on the degree of wickedness of the people. However if their hearts are hardened, woe unto them).

Note: These scriptures describe the Sons of Jacob as merciless killers who will destroy many people, if the Lord determines there is no possibility of repentance. However such mass killings are not without precedence, in the history of the tribes of Israel.

In ancient days the Israelites, after their exodus from Egypt, were instructed by the Lord to kill all people in many nations, and lands. These lands were to become the inheritance of Israel. In this warfare the Israelites were frequently commanded to kill every one, by the edge of the sword. The Lord considered the people thus destroyed to be terrible sinners. They were guilty of every moral sin imaginable, and the worship of false gods. However the disasters prophesied by the book of revelation may bring modern man into the depths of humility, which could be their salvation, from the "Sons of Jacob". Nevertheless they have been warned.

Our society today is no better than those anciently destroyed by the Israelites, or Sodom and Gomorrah destroyed by the Lord through fire rained down from the skies.

A young lion among sheep is a wonton killer and kills with impunity for the sheer excitement of the moment, and none can possibly stay his hand.

The Lord changed the name of the Patriarch Jacob to Israel. And Israel had 12 sons, by four wives, and these sons became the heads of the 12 tribes of Israel. Today these tribes have grown into nations. However there has been no attempt to maintain bloodline purity and many of the original twelve tribes have inter-married with other nations and peoples.

Through out the scriptures the term remnant, spoken in conjunction with "Jacob" or "Israel", refers to the bloodline of the 12 tribes of Israel, and to those, among the gentiles, who repent join the Church and through baptism, into the LDS Church, are adopted into the house of Israel.

Many members of the LDS Church, today believe that the Lamanites (see note 1), or Indians, the true aborigines of North and South America, are destined to become these terrible sons of Jacob.

We know from the Book of Mormon that Lamanites are descendants from Lehi, who was a descendant of Manasseh the first-born son to Joseph. But are all Spanish people Laminates? The answer is no.

Many Spanish-speaking people are of European descent and are gentiles and not Lamanites.

For example, immigrants, or conquers from Spain or Portugal who settled in South America are gentiles. Whereas the true aborigines of those South America nations are Lamanites, and therefore descendants of Joseph through his eldest son, Manasseh. They are Israelites.

And in those South America countries many of these Lamanites are considered second class citizens. They have even come to think of themselves that way and at present, many are ashamed of their roots. Then too they are dark skinned because of the curse put on their forefathers by the Lord for wickedness (See Ensign, article dated Sept 1972, entitled, "What is a Lamanite").

And consider the aborigines of Australia. I have seen pictures of them and some have blond hair and facial characteristics, not unlike any European, even though their skin is dark. And these aborigines appear to be isolated from white Europeans by many societal mores, and by personal preference on the part of the natives themselves.

All members of the house of Israel whether direct descendants (as maybe determined either by lineage descent or patriarchal blessing) are a remnant of Israel and all of these, in the general sense, are "sons of Jacob", either by blood or adoption, through baptism.

Moses in prophetic vision, anciently, records in Deut. 30:1-4 that if Israel does not follow the commandments of the Lord, they will be scattered to every corner of the earth, among all the nations, where they will be driven and abused, and lowly esteemed. And if they repent and are obedient to the Lords commandments . . . He will gather them . . . *"from thence will He fetch them"*.

The Israelites were disobedient and were scattered, . . . and they were driven, abused and lowly esteemed, and remain so to this very day, in fulfillment of the promise of the Lord.

So the gathering is, at present, a futuristic event. However the LDS Church through its missionary program is working on the enlightening and the gathering of all peoples, from all corners of the earth.

But who are these terrible Sons of Jacob? What tribe do they come from or are they remnants from the various tribes?

This point is made very clear by 3ʳᵈ Nephi, in verse 21:12, quoted above. Here Nephi states, *"And my people who are a remnant of Jacob . . . shall be among the gentiles, . . . as a young lion among the flocks of sheep . . . etc, etc"*.

Here the prophet 3rd Nephi identifies this "remnant of Jacob" as, "my people".

This prophet, 3ʳᵈ Nephi, was a descendant of Lehi who was a descendant of the 1ˢᵗ born son of Joseph, . . . whose name was Manasseh.

It would appear that these terrible sons of Jacob who may wreck such death among the unrepentant gentiles are the descendants of Manasseh of whom are also those called Lamanites in the book of Mormon.

And the reason they may perform this task of annihilation, is described in 1 Nephi 21:17. In this scripture, Nephi the

Prophet, prophesies to his Lamanite Brothers, *"Thy children shall make haste against thy destroyers; and they that made thee waste shall go forth of thee"*. These later generation descendants, . . . the children, . . . are to come up against those who "destroyed" and "wasted" them, or through force and might of arms abused, and subordinated, them and caused them to become an inferior people, and in that way "wasted" their lives.

These terrible "Sons of Jacob", will make this warfare against *"their adversaries, and all their enemies shall be cut off"* (3 Nephi 21:13). Those gentiles who may be thus destroyed are identified as the enemies of the Sons of Jacob.

These scriptures bring to mind the plight of the North and South American Indians. A very large group of people treated as second class citizens, for many generations.

In North America, and for as long as I can remember the "Indians", have been a people kept, by the US government.

A once proud, and independent people, who for many generations were, forced to live on reservations, with no consideration for their culture or rights.

Fed, housed and clothed by the government. Generation after generation have lived and died on the public dole.

If a current, or a future generation, among these people, were to become enlightened, and wake up to the injustices done to them over the generations they could very well be filled with anger, toward the gentiles.

I believe the same circumstances are applicable to the Indians of the South American nations, and else where in the world, such as the isles of the seas.

And then there is the matter of millions of illegal aliens, of Hispanic nationality, that are presently in this country. Since the Lord has dispersed "Israel" to the Four Corners of the earth

I would have to assume that even these illegal aliens have some of the blood of Israel flowing in their veins.

Especially those who have been "impressed and motivated" to make the dangerous and challenging trip to the USA, illegally, for the righteous reason of making a better living and supporting their families back home. Perhaps such a sacrifice bespeaks a higher motivation than material advantage alone?

These people originate from almost every major South American country. They migrate from their country of origin, first to Mexico and then come across the border, into the USA, under the leadership of "coyotes". This is the nickname for men who, for a price, lead people across the borders of the USA, covertly, and disperse them through the USA. Our government takes no action to stop this illegal immigration, because the major political party now in power benefits from this population largess in the form of voters.

Also these people take jobs that many Americans don't want. Jobs primarily in the agriculture industry. Back breaking, low paying work, in the fields. But to the illegal aliens the pay is better than "back home", and much is sent to family members. In fact these people send so much of their money to their families that for many South American countries this is a significant monetary resource, . . . and frankly they don't want to see it stop. So the governments of these South American countries speak to our political leaders and request that no border closure action is taken. And so far no action has been taken.

This very large group may also be the terrible "Sons of Jacob" that may wreck so much death and destruction in the near future.

Many of these souls have also found the LDS Church, both here, in this country, and in their home countries and have joined it and proven to be steadfast members.

From the "Lamanites" of the world will come the terrible sons of Jacob. They truly have an ax to grind, having endured generational circumstances that "destroyed and wasted" their lives, at the hands of gentiles, both in North and South America.

It is my personal opinion that if these Sons of Jacob are called upon to fulfill this dire prediction they will do so after the Saints have been removed to Missouri. I believe this because the exodus of the Saints is to occur before the devastation starts. And the "Sons of Jacob" may be active in their role when the cities are "broken up". When not even a car could escape the cities, because of broken up streets. (See 3 Nephi 21:13-14). At a time when physical destruction in the world has already commenced.

And when these "Sons of Jacob", have accomplished their task the Lord will bring them back into the fold of the tribes of Israel to be taught the gospel and to be given an inheritance in the lands of their origin, in a terrestrial world. (See 3rd Nephi 21:20-29). Why is the Lord so merciful to them? Perhaps because they have been "destroyed and wasted", by their enemies, for generations, and by then would have repented and are no longer under the burden of the sins of their Fathers.

The members of the tribe of Manasseh, who exodus to Zion, will be called upon to build up the New Jerusalem and its magnificent Temple acting under the direction of the tribe of Ephraim who received the richer blessings at the hand of Jacob. These "richer" blessings include the blessings of establishing

Zion in these latter days, the duties of Priesthood leadership and the holding of all keys and the blessing of all the people who gather to Zion. (See "Of the House of Israel", by Daniel H. Ludlow, 1991 January Ensign.)

Note 1: A Lamanite is a descendant of the two oldest sons of the Prophet, Lehi who were named Laman and Lemuel. These were rebellious and wicked sons and there descendants took upon themselves the name of Lamanites. Because of their wickedness these people were cursed with a dark skin. Laman and Lemuel, as the sons of Lehi are descendants of Joseph's oldest son, Manasseh. During their over 1000 year history, as recorded in the Book of Mormon, these people experienced a brief period of great righteousness then fell back into their wicked ways. (See Book of Mormon). Many of their descendants are the Indians initially conquered and horribly abused by De Soto, in the south lands of North America and Cortez, in South America.

The north American Indians were eventually conquered, and driven, by the gentile immigrants from Europe.

These Indians of both North and South America are the original inhabitants of these two great continents. And they are Israelites.

CHAPTER 4

BOOK OF REVELATIONS 8-11

This review of the last days as described in the Book of Revelations will be taken, in part, from the analysis put forth in "Millennial Messiah", by Elder Bruce R. McConkie, pages 382-388.

All of the events that are presented in this review are futuristic to present time but will occur before the second coming of the Lord, and are designed to prepare the earth for the coming of the Lord and the commencement of the Millennial period of the earth.

Revelation 8:1

This is the only scripture, I have found, that actually describes a starting time for the apocalypse.

However, in chapter 12 "Time Analysis", I provide a detailed description of Revelations 8:1 as the prophecy that provides the starting time of the apocalypse.

The scriptures, in chapters 8-11, that follow describe truly calamitous events and speak to terrible and destructive things that will befall the earth and its inhabitants following the time frame described in Revelations 8:1.

These, apocalyptic, events are a preparatory and cleansing process. A process designed to rid the earth of all wickedness, and prepare it for the Second Coming of the Lord and the millennial reign. These events are initiated by seven angels who each has a trumpet. The sounding of 6 of these angles will unleash on the earth terrible plagues, and the 7th a jubilation.

We will review, in summary form, each of the plagues as presented in this part of the Book of Revelations.

Revelation 8:7-the first angel

When this angel sounds, hail, and fire mingled with blood are cast upon the earth and the third part of all trees and all the green grass was burnt up.

(A destruction of so much plant life will have a terrible effect upon all animal life and ultimately upon man. Any hail that is so destructive as to destroy trees will most certainly tear flesh and brake bone caught in the downpour. Crashing trees and structures will cause power failures, electrical shortages, gas line breaks and fire. Extreme cold can destroy cell structure of trees and grass just as though they had been burned. Such a large concentration of freezing water as this hailstorm will be, may be accompanied by an ice storm that sucks moisture out of the atmosphere and encases trees and grass in many pounds of ice. This will be a hailstorm unlike anything ever experienced or even imagined).

Revelation 8:8—the second angel

When this angel sounds his trump a great mountain, as it were, burning with fire was cast into the sea and a third part of the sea became blood; and the third part of the creatures in the sea died, and a third of all ships at sea were destroyed.

(It may well be that a series of volcanoes or several mega-volcanoes will erupt spewing boulders, magma and ash, and pollute a large part of the sea and destroy all the creatures in that part of the sea, and cause it to appear as blood through contamination. Perhaps the devastation known as red tide. A volcano may arise from the depths of the sea. Think of the loss of food sources to man. Especially those who rely on the sea for a living. Also there would be huge oceanic tidelic action, caused by the large chunks of earth tossed into the seas by the volcanoes, that will devastate coastlines and destroy one-third of all the ships at sea).

Revelations 8:10—the third angel

When this angel sounds his trump, a great star falls from heaven, burning as it were a lamp, and it falls upon one-third of the rivers and fountains of water; And the name of the star is "wormwood", and men die because the waters are made bitter.

(Wormwood according to the Internet is available as an oil and is toxic, to man; however, in an herbal format it is used internally, in the body of man, to kill parasites. In this revelation John saw an asteroid body or a meteor falling to the earth, in a brilliant flame as it plowed through the atmosphere, which he interpreted as a star falling to the earth. And apparently this asteroid body will be loaded with this toxic substance. In this calamity a third part of the world's fresh water is contaminated and rendered undrinkable. Nevertheless, because of thirst man will try and use it and will die. This polluted water could also end up in fruits and vegetables. Today some of the water in Mexico, and other countries is contaminated and if drank out right or ingested can cause terrible diarrhea. Undoubtedly a large part of the global population will have to relocate, to areas where potable water is available. Also the destruction from the impact of such a large asteroid body or meteor would in it self be devastating. It occurs to me that a third of fresh water must be a very large body of water such as . . . perhaps the five great lakes in North America, and the Canadian border or Lake Baikal in Siberia).

Revelation 8:12—the fourth angel

And when this angel sounds his trump, a third part of the Sun, the Moon, and the Stars, are darkened, and the day shone for a third part of it and the night likewise.

(This is a terrible disaster of diminished light and warmth and is probably caused by the debris tossed up by volcanoes, and asteroids, which would block out the heat from the sun. Substantially reduced growing time, will lead to food shortages. And reduced warmth on the earth will result in a much colder climate. A very frightening time for man. Probably very much like the vapor of darkness the Nephites experienced for three days, at the coming of the resurrected Christ to this continent (See 3 Nephi:13).

Revelation 8:13—woe's to come

And another angel is heard saying with a loud voice, woe, woe, woe, to the inhabitants of the earth by reason of the other three angels which are yet to sound!

(This angel will actually be heard by the inhabitants of the earth. That should be an eye opener, for man. However many will have second thoughts and conclude that the "loud voice" was only a figment of their imagination. Up to this point in time the disasters have been devastation's involving nature, however this interim angel tells us of greater woes that are destined to befall man if man does not repent. Wars are going to follow that have the direct result of killing people and reducing population. The previous four angels have unleashed plagues that are a very strong call to repentance. However we are hear warned that the following plagues will kill the wicked and cleanse the earth).

Revelations 9:1—the fifth angel

The 5th angel opens the bottomless pit, from out of which comes:

32

Smoke—the smoke of a great furnace that darkens the Sun and the air.

Locusts—come out of the smoke, and are given power as the scorpions of the earth.

Scorpions—cannot hurt any thing green but can torment man five months, but not kill them. In those days man shall want to die but cannot.

Locusts—were like horses prepared for battle. Had crowns of gold on their heads. Their faces were the faces of men, their hair as the hair of a woman, and teeth as the teeth of lions.

Locusts—had breastplates of iron, and their wings had the sound of many horses running to battle. They had stingers in their tails and their power was to hurt man 5 months.

King Locust—they have a king over them who is the angel of the bottomless pit, and his name is Abaddon (Hebrew) and Apollyon (Greek), the destroyer, or Satan.

(In this revelation John saw war and armies with a leader. A very evil leader. He saw equipment that was unlike anything he had ever seen. Probably tanks, with men's faces looking out the steering ports, and cannons, and machine guns mounted on rotating turrets. And flame throwers, and bazookas, and mortars. He also probably saw Jet fighter planes launching rockets, and the white exhaust coming from the flame tubes. All implements of war. A war is engaged for a period of 5 months. Men who are maimed, crippled, and exhausted will want to die but cannot. This short war is designed to "hurt man". These conditions are to bring about circumstances that promote repentance. Once again the Lord extends one last opportunity to man to repent. There are a number of people among the wicked who will not take up the "sword" against their neighbors who must "flee unto Zion for safety" (See D/C 45:68). These people will apparently draw the line at killing and will have to flee. And the only place where they will be safe is in Zion (Missouri).

Revelations 9:10-21, & 11 the sixth angel

And the sixth angel loosed four more angels, from the bottomless pit (Angels of Satan) who oversaw the great army that destroys a third part of man. And this army had iron horses, with heads of lions and out of their mouths came fire and brimstone. And power was in their mouths and in their tails to do hurt, for a little over a year's time.

This army is huge, and numbers 200,000,000 (See Rev 9:16). And the rest of the men that were not killed repented not.

Jerusalem will be under siege, and about ready to fall, when two prophets will appear in the streets. These prophets have great power, and wage war with fire and hold the hordes at bay slaying many for the space of three and one-half years. Finally the two prophets are killed, and left lying in the streets and the hoards celebrate and dance around them, for three and one-half days then life comes back into the two prophets and they stand on their feet, and are lifted up into heaven.

Then a great earthquake kills seven thousand men, and the remnant give praise to God.

In this period, Christ with great power, has brought to pass the destruction of all enemies by fire and has brought to pass the change of the world from a telestial world to a terrestrial world. This last burning is the most destructive power and surpasses all other destructive powers.

(The 5-month war was a skirmish compared to the war that now follows. Those who will participate in this war are very wicked, indeed. They have resisted every effort the Lord has made to motivate them to repent. In many respects they are like the Lamanites and the Nephites whose hate was so great, they fought to annihilation. Never in the history of the world have so many combatants been engaged in battle. Devastation is huge, totaling one-third of all the men on earth. Apparently the battle will occur in the area of Judea, as Jerusalem itself is under siege and about to fall. The Jews are about to be exterminated by war, when the

Lord will call two prophets to assist in the fighting. These prophets will have extraordinary powers and will be able to inflict great destruction on this enormous army and hold it at bay. However eventually they will be killed. The enemy will be so jubilant over the death of these two prophets that they will leave their bodies in the streets for 3.5 days and the enemy will celebrate and dance in the streets and send gifts to one another. Then the prophets will stand up to the surprise and fear of the enemy and will then ascend into heaven.

And then the Lord will cleanse the earth by fire, killing off the remainder of telestial souls who will not repent and thereby cleanse the earth and make the final preparation for its terrestrial estate.

Peter the Chief Apostle, in 2 Peter 3:10 prophesies, *"But the day of the Lord will come as a thief in the night; in the which the heavens shall pass away with a great noise, and the elements shall melt with fervent heat, the earth also and all the works that are therein shall be burned up"*. Apparently the final devastating fire will come unexpectedly, but with a great noise. It very much sounds like a atmospheric conflagration, that melts the surface of the earth. I personally don't believe that this will be by nuclear bombs. Such bombs are a terrible pollutant. Our God, who can cause the earth to stand still, stop the dark of night from coming, flood the earth with water, and transport the earth from Kolob to its present nursery location in the twinkling of an eye; certainly knows what to do to baptize the earth by fire, without polluting the earth for 100 years or more. Just a large solar flare could melt the surface of the earth, without polluting the earth for 100 or more years. In its terrestrial state the earth will be pristine in every way. In any event this will be a fire completely controlled by the spirit as the fire will have no effect on any thing *"that is by the Lord"*. Nothing that has been blessed and consecrated by the Melchizedek Priesthood will be destroyed (See D/C 132:14).

As a forest fire reseeds the forest so will the "fervent heat" with which the earth is cleansed animate the growth of the seed for the terrestrial world that will arise out of the ashes of the telestial world. Seed that will produce trees and plants that will provide man with every food requirement, including protein. Their will be no killing of animals for their flesh in the Terrestrial world. And with this cleansing complete the Lord will come with His robes of red reminding those who remain of the blood He shed for them.

At the coming of the Lord a series of resurrections are initiated. The morning of the 1st resurrection for those dead who are celestial, and the afternoon of the 1st resurrection for those who are terrestrial. The resurrection for the telestial dead will not occur until after the one thousand years of the millennium and will be the largest resurrection by far.

I firmly believe that the earth will be relocated to a Terrestrial location within the galaxy, up in the spiral arms of pink. It will cease to be a blue planet. And then after a thousand years, it will be relocated near Kolob and become a planet of glory). (See the Kolob Theorem, by Lynn M Hilton Ph.D.)

Revelations 11:15-the seventh angel

When this angel sounds great voices are heard, from heaven, proclaiming that the kingdoms of the world have become the kingdoms of Christ.

(This angel has the happy task of initiating the jubilation that will announce to all that Christ is victorious and has destroyed all of His enemies. This will be a great day of rejoicing both on earth and in the heavens.

Satan is bound, because no one on the new Terrestrial world will listen to him. He is rejected totally and completely, until the end of the thousand years when he will once again have some success with man).

CHAPTER 5

DOCTRINE & COVENANTS, SECTION 29

This revelation was given to the Prophet Joseph Smith, in September 1830, in the presence of six Elders, given some days, prior to a Church Conference.

And is unique in that it is the word of the Lord to modern man. In this revelation the Lord speaks to my dispensation of time; He speaks to my day, and therefore to me.

In section 29 of the Doctrine and Covenants the Lord states in verse 8 *"That a decree has gone forth from the Father that they (mine elect) shall be gathered in unto one place to prepare them against the day when tribulation and desolation are sent forth upon the wicked".*

References to *"gathered",* makes reference through foot notes to the place called the New Jerusalem, which Mormons know to be the area called Jackson County, Missouri. So this part of the revelation is talking about a time, yet futuristic, when the Lord will initiate a gathering of His Saints to Missouri.

In verses 9-13 the Lord reveals the things that will befall the Saints, and the world after this gathering and He plainly states that the time is coming when the wicked will be burned up, when He will reveal himself, and the original quorum of 12 Apostles will stand with Him, and He will dwell with man for a thousand years, during the millennium.

These five verses are a summary of the Lords description of things that will come to pass, in time. They are designed to buoy the heart and encourage the saints to be steadfast, and to have faith. These are the days of joy that saints have longed for since the Church's inception . . . the Second Coming of the Lord.

Then in section 29 verse 14, He declares, *"But behold, I say unto you that before this great day shall come"* . . . and then He describes the frightening events that must transpire before He comes to earth, before that great day of His Second Coming. But after the Saints have been gathered . . . to Missouri.

When will the gathering "of the elect" . . . happen? This revelation makes no mention of timing in this last days events. That task was left up to the Lords Apostle, John the beloved, who recorded the great futuristic record known as the Book of Revelations as discussed in chapter 12 of this writing.

With the "elect" safely situated in Missouri the Lord will begin to cry repentance to the world, in a profound and unmistakable way.

The "cleansing of the earth" is not an arbitrary, or capricious action of destruction taken by the Lord. But a carefully orchestrated series of events designed to change the hearts of men, and bring them into the depths of humility.

He calls these events "tribulations and desolation's" (See note 2).

From this terminology one can only conclude that the experiences that follow are designed to humble man and bring him to repentance or destroy him.

These will be terrifying events, for those in the world, as the Lord will cry repentance unto the world as follows:

<u>Verse 14.</u> Sun shall be darkened . . . Moon turned to blood . . . stars shall fall from Heaven. And their will be signs in the Heavens and in the bowels of the earth.

(Multiple volcanoes, or mega-volcanoes (calderas), erupting around the world would put so much debris in the atmosphere that the sun would indeed be darkened and the Moon, through such a dark veil would certainly appear as blood. Accompany this with multiple earthquakes around the world, from the "bowels of the earth", and the associated debris and dust that goes with such cataclysmic events, and the situation is magnified several fold. But that is not all. He declares that stars will fall from Heaven. Asteroids will cause enormous damage and debris, all by themselves. (See also Revelations 8:8 and 8:10. that quantify the amount of destruction). Such terrible calamities could apparently cause the earth to *"reel to and fro"* (D/C 49:23). These events may occur, simultaneously, or in rapid succession. The earthquakes are actually restoring the earth to its original configuration (See D/C 133:22-24).

D/C 45:33 says, *"that there will be many earthquakes and many desolation's, and yet man will harden their hearts against the Lord, and will take up the sword against one another"*. And D/C 45:68, says *"and it shall come to pass among the wicked that every man that will not take his sword against his neighbor, must needs flee unto Zion for safety"*. Some people will flee to Zion for safety).

<u>Verse 15.</u> Weeping & wailing among men.

(Unquestionably it would appear as though the world is coming unglued and fear among men would be natural because of the hopelessness of the situation. The calamities of verse 14, create disasters that are well beyond the scope of any government or combination of governments to provide relief. People will be completely isolated. Destroyed homes will be little more than caves with no amenities. Also fear and isolation is a great motivator and may lead some in the world to repent.

In addition the nations have for years been experiencing wars and rumor of wars, which are also part of the call to repentance in our present day (See Teachings of the Prophet Joseph Smith, pg. 160). Many will be injured and killed from this global devastation.

Verse 16. Great hailstorm destroys the crops of the earth.

(Here is a disaster of major proportion. Because of all the debris thrown into the atmosphere by the 1st plague, increased volumes of water will be circling the globe. This water will fall through an atmosphere that has been cooled from the smoke ash and dust, that is blocking out the sun. The water will freeze and hit earth as large hailstones destroying much of the plant life. Global destruction of crops will cause a famine. (See Rev 8:7, that quantifies how much plant life will be destroyed).

Verse18. Flies shall eat the flesh of the inhabitants of the earth, and maggots will come upon them.

(Many people, and domestic live stock will have been injured, and weakened through famine, and many will have been killed outright. The injured may not have access to medical care. However with all the damaged plant life, and dead people and animals, the flies will be fairing very well and will be prolific, as in the days of the plague that, the Lord, through Moses, brought upon the Egyptians. Flies love carnage, and lay eggs in it and the eggs become maggots, and the maggots become more flies. Flies would be prolific).

Verse 19. Their tongues shall be stayed, and not utter against the Lord, flesh shall fall from off their bones, and their eyes from their sockets.

(This prediction has been made before and came to pass. In Zech.14:12, the Old Testament Prophet declared, *"And this shall be the plague where with the Lord will smite all the people that have fought against Jerusalem; Their flesh shall consume away while they stand upon their feet, and their eyes shall consume away in their holes, and their tongues shall consume away in their mouth"*.

"This prophesied plague will occur because the people refuse to repent. This plague may be caused by a new germ. A new microbe or a new bacilli, that the scientist have no experience with". (See Doctrine & Covenants commentary, by the Apostle Hyrum Smith and Janne M. Sjodahl, pg.152).

Verse 20. Beasts of the forests and fowls of the air will devour them.

(In such global disasters as described above carnivorous animals would flourish with the abundance of flesh. This is also the clean up crew).

<u>Verse 21.</u> The Great and Abominable Church to be cast down by devouring fire.

(This is the great Church of the Devil spoken of in 1 Nephi 13:5-9 and in Revelation 17. This great organization and all its properties are to be destroyed by a fire so intense that it is described as a *"devouring fire"*. When the fire is through nothing will remain, of the great and abominable church, not even brick, mortar and re-bar, . . . nothing).

The cleansing of the earth is so thorough that Doctrine and Covenants section 132:13-14, describes that *"nothing is to remain on the earth that isn't by the Lord"*. I imagine that this means peoples, or properties that have been blessed by the Priesthood of the Lord, will be the only things to survive the plagues.

In the meantime the Saints in Missouri will have been protected by the Lord and will be building up Zion, or the New Jerusalem. The Lord wants a new Temple built there. A Temple in which the Saints are commanded to present a book worthy of all acceptation. A record of their genealogies (see D/C 128:24).

One may ask? Why doesn't this revelation, in D/C 29, talk about the awesome task of the "Sons of Jacob".

The answer is, because this revelation is written to the members of the Lords church, who based on the Lords planning, will have the faithful safely tucked away in Missouri, where He will protect them, while the "Sons of Jacob" perform their task.

Also the revelations pertinent to the task of the "Sons of Jacob", was written specifically as a warning to the gentiles. Members of the Church are not gentiles.

Note 2: The word "tribulation", means severe affliction and prolonged suffering. The word "desolation", means to devastate and depopulate. Very frightening terms, with unique and specific objectives. The first is designed to promote repentance, while the latter is intended to remove population. First will come "tribulation" followed by "desolation".

Louis A. Kelsch

Why has it come to this? All my life the Lord has cried repentance to the world, through wars and events that we have described as natural disasters, that occurred because of the wickedness and greed of man. These were events that took life, . . . sometimes a lot of life. But rather than recognize them as calls to repentance, we just accepted these things as part of life. Had we repented years ago our earth today, most probably, would have been translated and become a Garden of Eden.

And we have the lessons of the past, . . . but we haven't learned from them. What did we learn from the wars of ancient Israel who was given power to destroy many kingdoms because those kingdoms were so evil? What have we learned from Sodom and Gomorrah? Nothing! We have learned nothing from the lessons of the past.

Satan has convinced many of the leading religionist of our day to refer to the Old Testament, that records many of the Lords dealings with men, . . . things that any prudent person can learn from . . . , as "folklore". By them, these lessons are treated as myths, or fables. Not lessons to be taken seriously. On one occasion I was told this to my face by a Pastor of a large protestant church, in the University district of Seattle Washington.

Satan has had great success with mortals and continues to do so. Satan is a spirit and can do nothing to mortal man accept through willing mortal servants. It is man that gives Satan his power and success.

The Lord is currently endeavoring to neutralize Satan by preaching repentance to man. If Satan has no mortal followers Satan has no power. But there are people in the world who refuse to repent. This leaves the Lord with no option but to destroy those who refuse to repent and hence, achieve victory over Satan. When Satan has no followers he is finished, "he is bound".

However he will have done great damage to man. He will have sabotaged eternal life (living in the presence of God) for many, many people. Satan is miserable and wants to make all of Heavenly Fathers children as miserable as he is.

Before the wicked reach the point of losing all opportunity for a degree of glory, . . . before their "cup of iniquity is full", the Lord will remove them from the source of temptation . . . mortality . . . and from the possibility of losing any chance for a kingdom of glory.

And so in the winding down scenes of this telestial estate in which we now live we hear words like tribulation and desolation spoken by He who has all power. However even these strong measures are in and of themselves a call to repentance. They are evidence that our marvelous God is doing everything in His power to save us in the best possible degree of glory. We have become the proverbial mule who was so obstinate that the only way the farmer could get his attention was to hit him in the head with a 2x4.

42

Tribulation and Desolation are going to be this worlds 2x4 . . . that will knock the unrepentant to their knees.

The earthquakes that will occur during these times of tribulation are "unprecedented", by any measuring standard.

In Helaman, in the Book of Mormon, we read of Samuel the Lamanite prophet who prophesied of the destruction that would occur on this hemisphere at the time the Lord would be crucified in Jerusalem. In Helaman 14:21-22 we read of the braking up the "solid mass" of the earth; *"Yea, they shall be rent in twain and shall ever after be found in seams and cracks, and in broken fragments upon the face of the whole earth, yea both above the earth and beneath".* Here we read of the creation of the tectonic plates at the time of the crucifixion of Christ. This revelation was given about 6 BC. However during the apocalypse the earth is to be renewed and receive its "paradisiacal glory". (see article of Faith #10). Paradisiacal glory means the glorified millennial state of the earth. The earth will be renewed to its Edenic configuration. Christ was crucified 32-34 AD and at the time the tectonic plates were created and have drifted apart ever since. However according to the scriptures they will be brought back together during the apocalypse. Such rapid movement of such a large mass would cause the earth to *"reel to and fro"* (see Psalms107:27, Isaiah 24:20, D/C 45:48, D/C 49:23 & D/C 88:87).

Revelations 16:18, records . . . *and there was a great earthquake, such as was not since men were upon the earth, so mighty an earthquake, and so great".* And then in Revelations 16:20 we read," *And every island fled away, and the mountains were not found".* Clearly John saw the same thing the Prophet Joseph Smith saw relative to the "renewing" of the earth, or the "restoration of all things".

CHAPTER 6

WHO ARE THE "ELECT"

The previous chapter's talk about "tribulations and desolation's" that are going to befall the wicked of the world after the "elect" have been removed to a safe place. For millennia the Prophets have looked forward to the last days and spoken about the redemption of Zion, . . . or the temporal salvation of the saints.

But who are the saints referred to in the Book of Revelations of the Holy Bible?

I submit that the saints referred to in this holy writ are the "elect" of the Church of Jesus Christ of Latter Day Saints.

The elect are those members of the Church who have spent their time in mortality trying to live the celestial law as put forth in all of revealed scriptures. The Old Testament, New Testament, the book of Mormon, Doctrine & Covenants, and the Pearl of Great Price. And the revelations from Prophets, Seers and revelators as published in Church media.

Our Prophets define "elect members" as those who hold the Priesthood, and have worked to magnify their callings in the

Priesthood. The "elect" are members of the Church who have been sealed to a wife and children in the temples of the Lord.

The elect are those who have endured all things for the sake of the Gospel of Jesus Christ up to the end. The "end" being their death or removal from the society of man.

Anyone in the world can become an "elect" saint if they wish too. The invitation is extended to all, and it is certainly not to late to do so.

Not all members of the LDS Church presently meet the standards for the elect. But those who are currently less valiant, at some point in time in their lives, have received a testimony of the truth of the Gospel. However, they presently struggle with the disciplines necessary to remember their original testimony and to be valiant in that testimony.

For example. Some years ago in the North Seattle Stake a visiting general authority told that congregation that if the Lord were to save only the full tithe payers of the Church, He would save only one-third of the Church. I have no idea if that's the case many years later. Tithing the preparatory law of the law of consecration, is for some merely a teething law of the gospel, but for others it is a stumbling block, or a rock of offense. For some it is an easy law, but for others it is very difficult. For some the word of wisdom, not using tobacco, liquor, or tea or coffee, is a rock of offense. For some accepting a calling in the Church, or several callings, as is frequently the case, . . . is a difficult thing to do.

Apparently the Lord will prune His Church before He permits any exodus, of the total congregation (see D/C 63:54). The reason being that those who are "casual" members of the Church need to be brought into the depths of humility, and come to a realization of how important their testimony is to them. They may have to experience some of the "tribulation" planned by the Lord.

This chapter will also focus on the Book of Mormon, 1st Nephi chapters 12-14. A review of these chapters of the Book of Mormon provide some back ground and sets the stage for the description of a church that will be in direct opposition to the saints and will make war against them at some point in time in the future.

These chapters, in the Book of Mormon, relate the experience of Nephi who prayed earnestly to have an understanding of the things that his Father had experienced. In answer to his prayer he was visited by, no less than, the Holy Ghost, who he reported *"was in the form of a man"* and, he was given a view of all generations of time relative to this earth, down to the last days. (See 1 Nephi 11:11).

Nephi saw the formation of the Church of the Devil, (See summary below) and noted that it was exceedingly wealthy and had world dominion.

He saw gentiles (European Immigrants) who were delivered by God out of the hands of all other nations, and were guided to a land of promise (North America). He saw that the mother gentile nation (Great Britain) from which the gentiles had fled, gathered to make war (revolutionary war) with the gentiles in this Promised Land. But the Lord blessed the gentiles in the Promised Land and they prevailed and, in time, were lifted up above all other nations.

These gentiles that came to the promised land brought a book (the bible) with them that taught about the Gospel of Jesus Christ but many plain and precious truths had been taken from it by the great and abominable Church. This book was a record they had obtained from the Jews.

Nephi saw that his descendants would become a dark and loathsome people, and the gentiles in the Promised Land would smite them but the gentiles would not utterly destroy his descendants (the Indians).

He saw a book taken to the Gentiles in the Promised Land that taught them the truth of the gospel of Jesus Christ in plainness (Book of Mormon). He reported that the Promised Land was blessed to be a blessing to those gentiles who worshiped the Lamb of God but it would be a cursing to those gentiles who rejected the teachings of the Lamb of God.

That brief review is a summary of 2 chapters and 65 verses, and brings us to chapter 14, of the Book of Mormon.

So in summary we have two large and powerful nations, referred to as gentile nations, who have subjugated the descendants of Nephi (the Indians).

Now we must understand that Nephi is talking about both the North American and the South American continents. In North America Nephi's descendants were subjugated, by the immigrant gentiles from Europe. His descendants in South America were subjugated by gentile conquerors from Spain and Portugal.

However the Promised Land that he reports as being the greatest of all nations; is North America.

And one of the things that has made this nation great is the constitution that the Lord provided the early founding Fathers of this nation, on July 4, 1776.

And then Nephi in the time frame 600 to 592 BC had a revelation from an angel that spoke to events that would occur just prior to the end of the world.

Nephi saw a time when there are only two Church's in all the world. He saw the Church of the Lamb of God and the Church of the Devil. He saw that the Church of the Devil *"had dominion over all the earth, among all nations, kindred's, tongues, and people",* (1 Nephi 14:10-11).

Nephi saw a time when there would be the church of the Devil and the church of the Lamb of God. And that the dominion of the Church of the Devil is global.

Nephi recorded that all of the people who did not belong to the Church of the Lamb of God belonged to the Church of the Devil (see 1 Nephi 14:10-11).

These are conditions that do not exist at the time of this writing but are futuristic to our present day.

Nephi saw that the dominions of the Church of the Lamb of God, *"who were the saints of God",* and their dominions were also upon the face of all the earth, but they were small.

He beheld that it came to pass that the Church of the Devil, *"did gather together multitudes upon the face of all the earth, among all the nations of the Gentiles, to fight against the Lamb of God"* (1 Nephi 14:13 and Rev. 13:7).

Nephi saw the Lord pour out His wrath upon the Church of the Devil, *"insomuch as wars and rumors of wars were poured out upon all the nations and kindred's of the earth"* (See 1 Nephi 14:15).

And then Nephi was informed, . . . that at the day when wars are poured out upon the earth, *"the work of the Father shall commence, in the preparing the way for the fulfilling of His covenants, which He made to His people who are of the house of Israel"* (See 1 Nephi14:17).

Summary

The term "the Church of the Devil", does not appear in the bible, it appears only in the Book of Mormon, and in the Doctrine and Covenants.

The LDS Church has identified the Church of the Devil as follows: "*The titles Church of the devil and great and abominable church are used to identify all churches or organizations of whatever name or nature-whether political, philosophical, educational, economic, social, fraternal, civic, or religious—which are designed to take man on a course that leads away from God and his laws and thus from salvation in the kingdom of God*", (see Mormon Doctrine, pg. 137).

The bible, on the other hand, uses the names "*Beast, Babylon, Mother of Harlots or Whore of all the Earth*" to define the Lords benchmark of evil organizations in the last days. However the most prominent of all these organizations in the Book of Revelations is the "Beast".

The Apostle John records in Rev 13:16-18, how, this world power designated "the Beast", will make war with the Saints. This world power will require everyone in the world to receive a mark in his or her hand or forehead. For simplicity let's call it a bar code on a card. And those who don't have it cannot buy or sell. They can't pay their property taxes, can't buy gas, can't buy groceries, or clothes, and can't pay mortgages. They can't pay utility bills, it's a total economic shut out. In order to qualify for the authorization to "buy" one must join with the "Beast".

Through revelation the LDS Church will know this is coming and before the "can't buy or sell" edict is issued the Church will encourage all its members to immediately live the law of consecration (See chapter 9, for Law of Consecration or United Order).

Many LDS members will bulk at this unprecedented level of sacrifice, and have second thoughts about their membership in the Church.

The Apostle John looking down through the corridors of time to the last days saw a world power that he identified as "Babylon the Great" and he referred to it as a harlot, who is *"drunken with the blood of the saints, and with the blood of the martyrs of Jesus"* (see Rev 17:5-6).

Which illustrates that in some locations persecution against the saints may be severe and in others it could be minimal or even non-existent. For instance on the East Coast and in very large cities on the West Coast, life for a latter day saint, may be intolerable. They will be forced to relocate or join the "Church of the Devil", or suffer persecution, or perish. Whereas in more remote areas of the west such discrimination is minimal or, may not exist at all.

This relocation of the "Elect" saints from the society of the world to more remote areas is the first exodus.

This persecution and exodus from the society of man, by the saints, is not with out precedent. In the meridian of time, history teaches us that, those early-day-saints "hid for fear of the Jews" and also for fear of the Romans.

The Priesthood leaders of the LDS Church will have everything in control. They will know where to go and what locations to avoid. Some members of the Church will have to relocate. Others may find themselves, temporarily, in "tent towns" at LDS Church recreational properties. For latter day saints it will be a very challenging and unsettling time.

This Babylon or Mother of Harlots, indeed, has a powerful ally in the world identified as the "Beast".

The Apostle John in Revelations 13:2 describes the "Beast". *"And the beast which I saw was like unto a leopard, and his feet were as the feet of a bear, and his mouth as the mouth of a lion: and the dragon gave him his power, and his seat, and great authority".*

This army is defined by symbols of "Beasts". I suggest that these symbols represent the following nations:

The Leopard I believe has reference to Africa. The bear to Russia, the lion to the Arab Nations, and the dragon to China. And apparently the dragon gives the combined army its "seat" or headquarters and its "authority".

This beast will have power for 42 months to exercise great control over the minds and hearts of man, and to make war against the saints. And all peoples on earth whose names are not written in "the book of life of the Lamb", shall worship the beast (see Rev 13:5-8).

This great "Babylon" (the Beast and the Church of the Devil) and its allies are rich. So rich that *"the merchants of the earth are waxed rich through the abundance of her delicacies"* (see Rev 18:3). Any society whose merchants are doing so well, certainly is not destitute, or brought to its knees by adversity. At least not yet.

And then the Lord, concerned that his saints may be tempted to partake of the wealth and sins of the "Harlot", will say: *"Come out of her my people, that ye be not partakers of her sins, and that ye receive not of her plagues"* (see Rev 18:4). In order to *"receive not of her plagues"*, the saints must exodus from the world and materialistic society of man. This exodus will be the second one and will be to Jackson, County Missouri.

By the time the saints are permitted to exodus, which will only happen when the Lord authorizes it . . . only the very faithful will remain in the Church. Those who have passed through the fire of persecution, by Babylon and its allies, are the "elect" and, will exodus to Missouri.

Considering the refining that the "elect ", must endure to qualify to exodus from the society of man, I shudder at the thought of what those who remain in the world, will endure after the "elect" are removed.

I believe that the "elect" will furnish the Priesthood leadership who will oversee the building up of "New Jerusalem", in Jackson County, Missouri.

When the Saints are finally led back to Missouri it will have been swept clean.

Brigham Young is reported to have said, something to the effect . . . *"When the Saints go to Missouri, their will not be so much as a stray yellow dog wagging its tail to greet them"*.

CHAPTER 7

PERSECUTION OF THE SAINTS

I wrote this chapter to explain, in more detail, my thoughts concerning experiences that I believe will befall the "Elect" in anticipation of the war the "Beast" will execute against the Church of the Lamb of God (LDS Church).

This war against the Saints is a purging or pruning action. It is very apparent to me that the Lord sanctions this refining of His Church. Through this purging action He will divide His church and remove the less faithful members. And those who remain will become His leaders and rulers for the Terrestrial world during the millennium. Those who remain faithful during these three and one-half years of persecution, by the "Beast" will be the first permitted to exodus to Missouri, and will be the "elect". They will be spared the horrible days of "tribulation and desolation", that will be unleashed on the world.

The Lord has revealed where the cleansing of the earth, preparatory to His Second Coming will begin.

"And upon my house shall it begin, and from my house shall it go forth, saith the Lord; First among those among you, saith the Lord, who have professed to know my name and have not known me, and

have blasphemed against me in the midst of my house, saith the Lord". *(D/C 112:23-26).*

In 1837, when this revelation was given, the Lord did indeed prune the fledgling LDS Church of apostates. Men who succumbed to the enticing of the adversary, who thought the Prophet Joseph Smith was not managing things properly, men who were critical of what was being done. In fact so pervasive was the evil intent of many in the Church, at that time, that the Lord sent Apostles to England, "for the salvation of my Church" (See History of the Church, Vol.11., pg. 489 & D/C Commentary, by Hyrum Smith & Janne M. Sjodahl, pg., 732).

The many convert Saints from England provided a steadying influence in the Church. However this was a strengthening of the Church, and not a cleansing.

Some of the saints in the 21st century are not so much vocal critics of the Church as they are simply unprepared and they are making no effort to meet the expectations of the Lord.

The Lord is no hypocrite. He will first cleanse His Church of the less valiant members, before He begins to clean the world of wickedness. As *"Many are called but few are chosen"* (See D/C 121:34-36).

I believe the Lord will begin the cleansing of His Church through the use of the Law of Consecration.

In Elder Russell M Nelson's April 2011 conference talk, titled, "Face the future with faith", he provided some very key thoughts. On page 3, 2nd paragraph he said, *"To develop enduring faith, an enduring commitment to be a full-tithe payer is essential. Then the tithe payer develops faith . . . to the point that tithing becomes a precious privilege".*

He concludes the 2nd paragraph with, *". . . tithing will keep your name enrolled among the people of God and protect you in the day of vengeance and burning"* (D/C85:3). And in the 3rd paragraph we read, *"Why do we need such resilient faith? Because difficult days are ahead"*.

Perhaps Elder Nelson is teaching that any member to whom the current law of tithing is painful, and is not instead a "precious privilege", may not have developed sufficient faith to accept the law of consecration.

In D/C 63:54 the Lord declares, *And until that hour there will be foolish virgins among the wise; and at that hour cometh an entire separation of the righteous and the wicked; and in that day will I send mine angels to pluck out the wicked and cast them into unquenchable fire.*

"Foolish virgins are those who feel that they can be less concerned about appearing before God than they would be, if they were being presented to a mortal monarch". (D/C commentary by Hyrum M Smith & Janne M Sjodahl, page 383)

In the revelation on "expectations of the Lord", as is recorded in D/C 58:26-29, the Lord concludes with the statement that *"he that doeth not anything until he is commanded, and receiveth a commandment with doubtful heart, and keepeth it with slothfulness, the same is damned"*. Damned meaning that progress, for the individual who behaves in such a manner . . . is stopped.

However the Lord, through his Priesthood leadership, is presently making every effort to give all members of the Church an opportunity to, "raise the bar" in their personal lives and, improve upon their faithfulness.

It would appear that the Lord is planning on a cleansing of His own house before He starts on the world. Such a cleansing will diminish the population of the LDS Church.

However those who successfully endure these trying days will become the people known as the "elect". They will become the leaders and rulers of the Terrestrial world that will arise from the ashes of the present day world.

But what will happen to those unprepared virgins that will constitute about one-half of the membership of the Church? They will become offended by the Church and will leave it and will embrace the world. Are they lost . . . for ever? The answer is no. But they may have to experience some of the "tribulation", of the cleansing of the earth process, to realize how important their testimonies were to them.

These less valiant people, at some point in their lives, were blessed with testimonies of the truthfulness of the LDS Church. A testimony of the Church can only be obtained by revelation from the Lord through the Holy Ghost. Their minds have been touched by a member of the God Head.

In addition for years they enjoyed the warmth and association of those who were valiant. They have heard their teachings, their testimonies, and have seen their example. They have been blessed with a more perfect knowledge of the truthfulness of the gospel. And they have failed to fully appreciate the full import of all these things and took these manifestations for granted, and failed to receive all things with a "contrite spirit and a broken heart". They are good people, by the standard of the world, but do nothing save they are commanded and receive such commandments with a doubtful heart. As a consequence they have no "oil in their lamps".

Just as the world during the "Apocalypse" is going to be forced to choose good or evil, so too will the saints be given this same option. However the saints will have their "challenge" in a society that will appear to them to be . . . normal. As the tribulation phase of the apocalypse will not yet have begun.

In each of the congregations, of the Latter Day Saints, there are those in our Wards and Stakes who I refer to as the "phantom congregations".

Most of this group seem to be content to be members in name only. I have met a number of them and . . . I liked them. They are basically good people, and good neighbors. Many won't come to church on the Sabbath or pay tithes but they will occassionaly join in on a work project or a sports activity; and also help out in the local soup kitchen.

At some point, in their lives, they were touched by the Holy Ghost, and converted. However over the years they have forgotten these feelings of conversion and succumbed to the world. However they remain baptized members of the Church and as such are of the house of Israel.

Chapter 2 of this book makes the point that all members of the house of Israel will be given the opportunity to repent and return to the LDS Church and be saved and protected through the process of "Restoration of all things".

It appears the Lord will give these inactive members, and indeed all the rebellious of the house of Israel, a second and final chance, before cleansing the earth by fire. But many will have to experience the frightening days of "tribulation", to fully appreciate just how important their testimonies are to them.

Isaiah, in prophetic vision, saw the refining of the Lords Church in the latter days. He saw the great affliction, and the abuse that the Lords Church would endure. He also saw how the tormenters of the Saints would come to feel about their participation in this abusive behavior. The remorse that they would come to feel in time; that would motivate them to make amends.

"The sons also of them that afflicted thee shall come bending unto thee; and all they that despised thee shall bow them selves down at the soles of thy feet; and they shall call thee, The City of the Lord, The Zion of the Holy One of Israel" (Isaiah 60:14).

Of this passage in Isaiah Cleon Skousen in his book "Isaiah speaks to modern man", pg. 721, declares:

"The prophets have indicated that just prior to the redemption of Zion, the Saints will suffer bitter persecution so that only the most faithful will survive as members of the Church. Many of those who ridiculed and persecuted the Saints will come to plead for their forgiveness. As their are some people who do not recognize the truth until history catches up with them. That is why those who know the truth can afford to be patient".

History has proven that the most vicious enemies of the Church have been apostates; those who were once one of us. A former Bishop of mine once said, *"I would rather face an angry mob of Protestants than a mob of apostate Mormons".*

Isaiah continues in 60:15, to make reference to the "elect" of the latter days, *"Where as thou hast been forsaken and hated, so that no man went through thee,* (reached out) *I will make thee an eternal excellency, a joy of many generations".*

Of this verse in Isaiah, Skousen reports, *"By way of comfort to the Saints during their time of persecution; Isaiah promises that if they will endure these hardships valiantly, the day will come when, the*

Lord will reward them in "eternal excellency", and they will become the pride and "joy of many generations".

There is a comforting thought in all of this for those of the Church who are determined to be faithful. And that is, . . . Isaiah speaks of them in the past tense, relative to the events of persecution.

Meaning of course that many will make it through the period of persecution. How can they not, succeed? They are on the Lords business. However for their faithfulness they will be richly blessed.

The "elect" experience

One thing is certain in my mind. The first casualties of the cleansing of the earth will be the faithful members of the LDS Church. They will be forced to flee, or go to prison or worse. They will become fugitives, . . . exiles from the society of man.

Three and one-half years of being a fugitive, on the run, from the armies of the "Beast" will strip the "Elect" of all materialistic inclinations, and serve to make them "more fit for the kingdom".

Their determination to be faithful in the face of such over whelming odds will merit the close association of the Holy Ghost. Persecution and hardship will make them physically stronger. They will come to rely almost completely on the spirit of the Lord. The over all health of these Saints will improve.

The first year, "in exile" will be challenging as the "elect", learn to cope with the task of obtaining the necessities of life. However, learning and adapting will come fast. These elect are the Terrestrial world leadership, in training, and they will be enrolled in a survival school.

Apostate members of the Church will tell the armies of the "Beast" where the Churches recreational properties are all located. So these camping sites will become traps and snares. The "Beast" will want to keep the faithful on the run, and off balance, to wear them out and force them to surrender, and join with the "Beast".

I imagine that captured fugitives, especially well known leaders of the Church, will be worth their weight in gold to be paraded before the public, in media propaganda to reinforce and illustrate the failure of the Church of the Lamb of God.

By the second and third year the faithful will have become skillful "survivors", and acclimated to the difficulties of being fugitives.

I would expect that the "Elect" will not hide underground like moles, but will be involved in strengthening other members, of the LDS Church and making new converts, of which there will be a few . . . as the Lord will save the honest in heart. These faithful will be the only missionaries in the world, and will receive their assignments from, Priesthood leaders, or the Holy Ghost, just as the faithful saints did in the meridian of time as they also stayed in "hiding for fear of the Jews". Communication will be very limited, for the "Elect" in their exile. They will come to rely on the Holy Ghost, and thereby become very conversant with revelation.

The 3.5 years will seem to go by very quickly for the "Elect".

The Lord has decreed that the "Beast" will have power to make war against the Church of the Lamb of God for only 3.5 years. So, by the middle of the 4th year the armies of the "Beast" will begin to relent, as the few remaining faithful Saints are too hard to find and to few in number to be bothered with. The "Beast" will conclude that the Church of the Lamb of God is no more. Their churches are all boarded up and no public meetings are being held. The "Beast" will even conclude that the Saints in prison are no threat and can be released. After all what can so few do? They have no standing in the community, and no possessions. The few remaining saints are vagabonds, and beggars. They will eventually be assimilated into the Church of the devil or die of natural causes . . . they are no longer a threat to the Church of the devil.

The "Beast" will probably remove the economic restriction on the world. Then fearing that the "Elect" may be tempted to partake of the wealth of "Babylon", the Lord will say, *"Come out of her my people . . . be not partakers of her sins"* (See rev. 18:3-4).

Obedient to this instruction the Saints, and their converts will commence the exodus to Missouri.

They, will openly travel the highways and byways to Missouri under the physical protection of the Lord. The Lord will go before them and be their rearward just as He did for the children of Israel in their exodus from Egypt. Nothing will hurt them or make them afraid in their exodus to Missouri.

And where will the faithful Saints, and their converts exodus from? From every corner of the earth. The Lords promise of one-half hour of silence in heaven is over, and the faithful Saints are safe in Missouri.

The cleansing of the earth . . . the days of "tribulation", followed by "desolation" will soon begin.

Chapter 8

WARNING

(Note: A smaller version of this chapter was offered to The Tacoma News Tribune and the Kansas City Star newspapers for publication in the religion sections of those papers. It was never published.)

The subject of the "Last Days", has become a subject of interest in our society of late. I attribute this to the report that the Mayan calendar ends Dec 21, 2012, and speculation is running high that this event coincides with the end of the world.

CNBC recently ran a 1 hour program titled, "Apocalypse 2012", and, at the time, had an on-going program titled "Doomsday Preppers" that describes the efforts many are making to prepare for an apocalypse. Apparently there is an ever-increasing interest in this subject.

To the Christian the term "The Last Days", speaks to the cataclysmic events associated with the second coming of the Lord Jesus Christ, as prophesied in the book of revelations of the Holy Bible.

With all due respect to the Mayan calendar, I believe that our very own scriptures are very clear as to the time when the

Lord will commence the cleansing of this earth of all evil, in preparation for His second coming.

For example, in the Book of Revelations, King James version of the Holy Bible, Chapter eight verse one, the Lord reveals to the Apostle John when the horrible events of the cleansing of the earth will begin. Revelations 8:1 says, *"And when He had opened the seventh seal, there was silence in Heaven about the space of half an hour"*.

The "He" in this verse is the Lord. The "seventh seal", has reference to the year 2000, which is the beginning of the 7000th period of time, and, I believe, the term "silence", means that the Heavens, or Deity, will not intervene in the affairs of man anymore than we have experienced to date, for that one-half hour period of time. In short both the principled and the unprincipled among us can continue to pursue our endeavors as usual, and we will not be influenced by God, anymore than is presently experienced, for that one-half hour period of time.

The term "one-half hour", is of special interest and is the key or code word to the timing when God will cease to be silent. If this term means one-half hour of mortal time it is meaningless, to me, because many one-half hour periods have come and gone since the year 2000 began. However if this one-half hour is Gods time, then that is an entirely different matter. So how long is Gods one-half hour? To calculate this we must understand Gods reckoning of time.

The chief Apostle Peter, in 2 Peter 3:8 states, *"But beloved, be not ignorant of this one thing, that one day is with the Lord as a thousand years, and a thousand years as one day"*.

So there it is, . . . Gods reckoning defined by the chief apostle. One of Gods days is equal to 1000 of our years. Divide

1000, or one of Gods days by 24 hours and we get 41.66 of our years, which represents one of Gods hours. Then divide 41.66 by 2, and we get 20.83 of our years that represents one half-hour of Gods time. Let's round that up to 21 years for a little latitude in timing. Add that to the year 2000 and you come up with 2021. (see Millennial Messiah by Elder Bruce R McConkie, page 382)

Isn't that a coincidence? The Mayan calendar ends 2012. Perhaps the Mayan's got the last two digits reversed?

Its my guess that in the year 2021 Heaven will no longer be silent, and that the horrible plagues that are described in the verses of the book of Revelations chapter 8 through 11 (see also chapter 4 of this book.) will start in that year.

What John describes are truly cataclysmic events, and horrible to imagine.

The destruction, described in these scriptures, seems to come in three phases. The first phase could best be described as tribulation, or unprecedented damage, and appears to be designed to promote repentance.

Then there is a second phase that follows that is best described as devastation, and is worldwide war that will reduce population.

The third phase is apparently global conflagration. Nothing is as final and cleansing as fire.

The underlying theme of the Book of Revelation is to rid the world of sin. The horrible events of destruction and the ensuing warfare that "depopulates" is to rid the world of those who refuse to repent.

Many people I speak to believe that our society is very wicked and expect God to punish us but they hope it won't happen in their lifetime.

We don't follow Gods laws and for the most part, . . . as a world society, we are a law unto ourselves.

The majority of us want God in our lives, . . . but on our terms. We have forgotten that God sets the terms we don't.

Besides Gods laws ask us to make sacrifice and the sacrifice He asks really isn't part of our comfort zone.

Well, for better or worse, it appears that our very own Christian scriptures may give us until 2021 to prepare to meet the end of our world as we know it.

Many people think the book of revelations is just folklore and won't really come to past, but do we want to bet our lives on it? Just suppose its intent is . . . a warning?

However . . . it is certainly true that the one sure way to neutralize Satan is to destroy all of his followers, which is pretty much the gist of the Book of Revelations.

Many believe that underground bunkers and the like will save them. That's like the people in the days of Noah, setting out in a rowboat when the floods came.

Based on our present experience with natural disasters, divinely sponsored destruction wouldn't cause us to repent unless it is unprecedented by any measurement standards we know of, or have experienced.

In other words, disasters on "a business as usual scale" won't produce repentance. Such disasters haven't filled the Church's yet. Why should we suppose that more of the same will cause a change?

The devastation prophesied in the book of revelations appears to be a judgment of our society, and it's not pretty.

Are we really so guilty of offending Deity? What is the judgmental yard stick of behavior that is so incriminating?

Just compare the Mosaic law (10 commandments) to our modern day commandments as contained in the New Testament.

The Mosaic law was given to the children of Israel, who had been slaves to Egyptian rulers for 400 years and as a result had lost much of the ability of self-government. Therefore God gave them a strict "school master". The penalty for breaking the Sabbath was death (Exo 31:14-15), for committing adultery also death, (Lev 20:10) and for homosexuality also death (Lev 20:13). If God permitted an ancient Israelite to be put to death for breaking His law . . . do we really think we are going to get a free pass for the same sin?

The "gospel of Jesus Christ" is our current divine law, and is adapted for a more enlightened people, and comes with a much, higher divine expectation than was expected of those who lived under the Mosaic Law.

For example the Mosaic law says "thou shalt not commit adultery". The gospel of Jesus Christ says . . . "if you think adulterous thoughts you are as guilty as if you committed adultery. (Matt 5:28).

This is a huge change in divine expectations. And even more basic than the law of adultery is the law to keep the Sabbath day holy. And can anyone remember the last time the shops and stores all closed on Sunday out of respect for the Sabbath? And haven't we all heard that church attendance is down?

What's more the scriptures make the point that if we disobey the laws of the gospel punishment is suspended to give the sinner an opportunity to repent. However we are promised that if the sin is not repented of a penalty will be exacted.

The threat of future penalties don't really seem to promote much change. After all, we cut our teeth on credit. Enjoy now and pay later is a way of life for us.

I think it's reasonable to conclude that we don't live the simple and basic Mosaic law let alone the gospel of Jesus Christ.

The basic theme of the gospel of Jesus Christ centers around the principle of repentance and "sacrifice"; basically the sacrifice of our sins.

One way to view the pending Apocalypse . . . Based on the scriptures, we may have just a few years to get in the good graces of the creator of this planet.

One thing is certain . . . and I think we can all agree . . . we have to quite ignoring God and take Him seriously . . . very seriously.

CHAPTER 9

LAW OF CONSECRATION

A ll members of the LDS Church are presently asked to pay an honest tithe. Tithes are defined as one-tenth of an annual income. Tithes are also a preparatory law to, a higher law known as, the Law of Consecration. Full compliance with the law of consecration is a principle taught by the Lord throughout the annals of time. I believe compliance with this law is an eventual test of faith and sacrifice that will be asked of the members of the Church.

This law has been lived or attempted through out the History of the world and has been called by various names; "Order of Enoch", "All things in common", "United Order", "Law of Consecration" and finally "Welfare Plan". For example:

★ About 3000 years BC It was called "The Order of Enoch". This attempt to live this principle under the Priesthood leadership of Enoch, was so successful the entire community, including the land on which it stood, was taken off the earth and translated to a Terrestrial level of being. (See Pearl of great Price, Moses 7)

* Then about 35-40 AD (Anno Domini) this principle was practiced under the Priesthood authority of the Apostles, and was known as "Having all things in common". This attempt was not completely successful as we learn from the story of Ananias and his wife Sapphira (Acts 5:1-11) who tried to cheat the system.

* Later in our dispensation, about 1831, it was practiced as the "United Order" under the leadership of the Prophet Joseph Smith and it failed because of the "greed and avarice" of man, . . . so the Lord waived part of the law and today requires that members of the Church now consecrate only a portion of their substance called a tithing.

* Later in the early 1900's it was practiced by the Church, but only partially, as the "Welfare Program of the Church", and that part has been an on going success ever since.

This law is one of the most pivotal laws in the entire mortal experience of mankind.

The bases of this law is plainly defined by the Lord in His 1st and 2nd great commandments; "*To love the Lord thy God with all thy heart, and with all thy soul, and with all thy mind. . . . and the second is like unto it, thou shalt love thy neighbor as thy self*" (see Matt 22:37-39, Mark 12:30-31, Luke 10:27 & D/C 59:5).

This commandment is the epitome of the law of consecration, and asks for a completely selfless person. One who loves God more than self and loves others just as much as self.

This commandment illustrates the sum and substance of the law of consecration and the expectation of the Lord.

In effect to consecrate something to God is to make it His. However it should be noted that such action is more for the benefit of the individual; for in point of fact since . . . God is who He is, . . . all things including our world, the Sun, our lives literally everything already belongs to God. By making some form of worshipful gesture, of giving, we exercise the principle of faith, and are taught obedience, and consequently improved upon. We draw closer to God.

However history has proven that the individual who acquiesces to God as fully and completely as He asks is rare. And yet it is a necessary principle, that will one day be expected, of the faithful, to practice, in the flesh, to qualify for eternal life.

The Lord has been very forth coming through out His association with man, whether in His role as Jehovah of the old testament or Jesus Christ of the New Testament and modern times, . . . and has revealed exactly what is expected of man to return to the presence of God the Father.

If this message is lost on us it is because we are so imbued with worldly affiliations that we fail to learn.

The new testament records an interview that Jesus had with a rich young man which I will paraphrase.

It seems a young man came running to the Lord one day and kneeled to Him and asked *"Good master what shall I do that I may inherit eternal life"* Where upon Jesus quoted him the required litany of obedience, i.e.: *"do not commit adultery, do not kill, do not steal, do not lie, do not defraud, honor your Father and Mother"*. The young man then replied, *"master all these have I observed from my youth"*.

Then Jesus looking on the young man loved him, and gave him the law of consecration.

He told the young man, *"One thing thou lackest; go thy way, sell whatsoever thou hast, and give to the poor, and thou shalt have treasure in heaven: and come, take up the cross and follow me"*. The young man had just received a promise of eternal life if he would live the law of consecration from He who has the keys to the eternities. The young mans response was both sad and telling. *"And he was sad at that saying and went away grieved: for he had great possessions"* (see Mark 10:17-22).

In this story we see an obedient young man who had faithfully practiced the law of Moses confronted with the law of consecration and he "stumbled". He knew he could not measure up to this last commandment and that made him sad. So he went away from the Lord, which is a shadow of things many will experience in mortality who are equally obedient.

In point of fact if we understand the parable of the ten virgins correctly; fully fifty-percent of the members will one day also *"walk away from the Lord grieved"*.

Lets consider another story. One day Jesus sat at the treasury and observed how people cast money into the treasury: and how many that were rich cast in much. And then along came a poor widow and she threw in two mites which add up to a farthing.

Jesus immediately saw this as a teaching moment and called His disciples to him and said; *"Verily I say unto you, that this poor widow hath cast more in, than all they which have cast into the treasury: for all they did cast in of their abundance; but she of her want did cast in all that she had, even all her living"* (see Mark 12:42-44).

When one casts in of his abundance he makes a contribution. When one casts in all her living she lives the law of consecration.

After the crucifixion of the Lord, the apostles initiated the practice of the "United Order" as recorded in Acts 4:32-37. In these scriptures we learn that the saints believed *"with one heart and of one soul: neither said any of them that ought of the things that they possessed was his own; but they had all things common".*

These verses reveal that only in an environment of complete unity, of mind, can the united order be successful.

The scripture continues and illustrates the fruits of such a successful effort.

"Neither was there any among them that lacked: for as many as were possessors of lands or houses sold them, and brought the price of the things that were sold, and laid them down at the Apostles feet: and distribution was made unto every man according as he had need".

In this example we see revealed the true purpose of the law of consecration. To ensure that there are no poor among them. To have such a condition among faithful believers, who *"believed with one heart and of one soul"*, is truly the living of a celestial law. The participants were living celestial law in a telestial world and undoubtly experiencing the joy and spiritual manifestations associated with that law.

Clearly, as a people, we cannot live celestial law unless there are "no poor among us".

Their was a couple named Ananais and his wife Sapphira who made a pact together to cheat the system. They sold a property and only laid part of the price at the feet of the Apostles, but certified they had laid it all. They lied. And for their lie the spirit took their lives (see Act 5:1-10). A harsh lesson. Apparently we mortals tend to forget that God knows our very thoughts. Both uttered and unexpressed. Also this is a lesson for all who accept the "Law of Consecration". *"Where much is given much is expected".* When the Lord settles celestial blessings upon those who agree to live the law of consecration, we must remember that all such agreements come with a *"covenant and a deed" which cannot be broken"* and are binding agreements.

From the foregoing we learn that our God has been teaching and advocating compliance with the law of consecration since the days of antiquity.

Divine commandments and expectations are no different in this last dispensation of time.

On Feb 9, 1831 the Prophet Joseph Smith received the revelation now known as Doctrine & Covenants 42:30-39. In verse 30 the Lord stated, *"And behold thou wilt remember the poor, and consecrate of thy properties for their support that which thou hast to impart unto them, with a covenant and a deed which cannot be broken".*

In verse 31, the Lord declares, *"And inasmuch as ye impart of your substance unto the poor, ye do it unto me; . . . etc?* The Lord wants the poor remembered for His sake.

These verses describe the mechanics of the working of the law of consecration which can be summarized as follows:

1. An individual signs all of his property over to the church.
2. The Bishop then returns to him that which he needs to support himself and his family, and makes him a steward over, what is now, the church's property.
3. Any surplus resulting from this action is given to the poor.

It occurs to me that many people working in common cause can produce much more than any individual going it alone. And would indeed produce much more "surplus", and thus benefit all in the order.

The principle ingredient for such a venture to succeed would be an unwavering commitment to equality in all things.

In today's society we extol the entrepreneur. If he is successful he will live in a much nicer home, drive a much nicer car and be materially elevated over his neighbor. This illustrates the principle of self reliance.

In the united order the entire group benefits from diligent work and if the surplus is sufficient everyone in the group prospers the same. All are, . . . and remain equal.

However there is an added edge to those who live the law of consecration, under the direction of the Priesthood of the Church, in that they live a celestial law and will be blessed by the Lord accordingly. Their initiative and enterprise will have the edge of divine guidance, and blessings, ensuring success.

The purpose for this encompassing law of charity is very interesting as is recorded in D/C 42:35-36.

Not only was the purpose pertinent to the needs of the day and also relative to building houses of worship, but also *"and building up the New Jerusalem which is hereafter to be revealed. That my covenant people may be gathered in one in that day when I shall come to my temple. And this I do for the salvation of my people".* Apparently this same law of charity will apply in the day for the *"building up the New Jerusalem",* in a day when the covenant people will be gathered, and *"in that day when I shall come to my temple",* in the day of the second coming of the Lord. Obviously an event as yet futuristic to our present day.

Here the Lord speaks of gathering His covenant people to the New Jerusalem. And even though they have entered into a temple covenant they are presently under no greater obligation than the law of tithing, which is a preparatory law to the law of consecration.

As a people we have not yet been tasked to prove our faith to the law of consecration. So that challenge is yet before us.

The LDS Church tried to live the law of consecration, or united order, during the years 1831 through 1834, and failed because of greed and avarice. The Lord issued a sharp rebuke in D/C 105:3-5, in 1834 over this failure, and instituted the law of Tithing as a preparatory law to the law of consecration in 1838 (see D/C 119).

However it should be noted that the celestial law of consecration must one day be lived in its fullness, *"And Zion cannot be built up unless it is by the principles of the law of the celestial kingdom; otherwise I cannot receive her unto myself"* (see D/C 105:5). The Zion that is to be built up, the one where the Temple that the Lord will come to, doesn't exist at present.

When the church will be asked to live the law of consecration is a time and circumstance, *"hereafter to be revealed"*.

Our Prophets are doing their best to encourage us to be faithful in the paying of tithes knowing that tithing is the preparatory law to the law of consecration.

In the June 2011 Ensign President Eyring provided a home teaching lesson called. "The blessings of Tithing". In this article he declared, *"One of the blessings that comes from paying a full tithing is developing faith to live an even higher law. To live in the Celestial Kingdom we must be able to live the law of consecration. There we must be able to feel that all we are and all we have belong to God"*.

Earlier in the year, in the April 2011 conference, Elder Russell M Nelson, in his talk titled "Face The Future With Faith", said; *"To develop enduring faith, an enduring commitment to be a full-tithe payer is essential"* . . . *To the point that tithing becomes a precious privilege* . . .

Why do we need such resilient faith? Because difficult days are ahead. Rarely in the future will it be easy or popular to be a faithful Latter-Day-Saint. Each of us will be tested. The Apostle Paul warned, that in the Latter Days . . . *, those who diligently follow the Lord* . . . *"shall suffer persecution".*

Our modern day prophets are encouraging us to be more diligent in preparing to live the law of consecration.

When will we be asked to live the law of consecration? The answer to this question is *"at a time hereafter to be revealed"*. At present we don't know.

We do know that in the "last days" an army designated by the Lord as the "Beast" spoken of in chapter 7 will have the power given it to test and try the saints.

Perhaps these are the very things Elder Russell M Nelson had in mind when he said *"difficult days are ahead of us"* and *"each of us will be tested"*. And *"Rarely in the future will it be easy or popular to be a faithful Latter-Day-Saint"*. (See Russell M Nelson talk "Face the future with faith").

However I am persuaded that living a higher law, whether popular or not, will bring with it the joy and happiness associated with a higher level of righteousness. I am persuaded that the saints who live the law of consecration will be the happiest people on earth, regardless of the threat of persecution. To me this means greater spiritual manifestations, and insights. Greater levels of understanding and achievement. Greater success in the saving of souls. Improved health, strength, and mental acuity. In effect everything in ones life would be improved to celestial standards. The law of the harvest is immutable, . . . live a law and reap a blessing.

Perhaps the living of the law of consecration will carry us through *"the tests"*, that lie ahead.

I submit that just as the early-day-saints of this dispensation through the law of consecration and their great faith, established the Church in the "tops of the mountains"; so will the last-days-saints, of this dispensation, through their faith in the law of consecration establish the church in Jackson County, Missouri . . . "the New Jerusalem".

And so at a time *"yet to be revealed"* the saints, and the world, will have the opportunity to choose to follow the Lord or Satan.

It is also very clear to me that, in these "last days" and more so than ever, we must never be "casual" about heeding the counsel of our prophets. The words they speak under the inspiration of the spirit are revelation from the lord.

If you would be saved in the winding down scenes of our society, make sure *"the payment of tithes is a precious privilege"*.

And remember the time is short. We are already in our 13th year into the 7,000th period of time; of the millennial period, in which the Lord is to come and initiate His terrestrial reign (see D/C 77:12).

CHAPTER 10

SIGNS

The purpose of this chapter is to explore the possibility of signs occurring in our society that point to a societal entity known as the "Church of the Devil" who is destined to have dominion over the world immediately prior to the days of the apocalypse.

The Book of Mormon, 1 Nephi 14:10-11 describes an entity who is prophesied to be the ruling authority of the world prior to the cleansing of the earth, of all wickedness, and prior to the second coming of the Lord Jesus Christ.

Verse 10 declares, *And he said unto me: Behold there are save two churches only; the one is the church of the Lamb of God, and the other is the church of the Devil; wherefore whoso belonged not to the church of the Lamb of God belonged to that great church, which is the mother of abominations; and she is the whore of all the earth.*

Verse 11 declares, *And it came to pass that I looked and behold the whore of all the earth, and she sat upon many waters; and* <u>*she had dominion*</u> <u>*over all the earth, among all nations, kindred's, tongues and people.*</u>

To my mind these verses in their literal interpretation describe a time, in the future, when a Church . . . a religious entity that the Prophet Nephi refers to as the Church of the Devil will have dominion over all the earth and everyone, in the world, will belong to one of two churches. The Church of the Devil and the Church of the Lamb of God.

Bear in mind that the word "dominion", means *territorial sovereignty*, . . . (New Webster Dictionary.)

The terms, "Church of the Devil, or "Great and Abominable Church" have been defined by the Church of Jesus Christ of Latter Day Saints as set forth in chapter 6 under sub-heading "summary."

This quote, to my understanding is the official position of the LDS Church on Book of Mormon scriptures, 1 Nephi 14:10-11.

So as the last days approach and our society rapidly diminishes in matters, moral and spiritual, political, and respect for the rule of law, one is left to ask who is this great church that will rule the world? Where are the signs of its evolution as a societal leader prior to the cleansing apocalypse that the Lord will unleash upon the earth, before His Second Coming?

In the spirit of the LDS Church's definition, of Church of the Devil, referenced above I submit several personal opinions on this matter that I suggest as potential scenarios.

Scenerio#1

When I read these same Book of Mormon scriptures in early 1950 I assumed that those conditions, described by these verses, had existed since the organization of the LDS Church, on April 6, 1830, and had reference to all the Churches that came out of the apostasy of the church that the Lord organized in the meridian of time. I did not look upon the meaning of these scriptures as being literal, but rather as referring to a conglomeration of world wide Churches, that called themselves "Christian Church's", and seemed to always be in competition for the souls and hearts of men.

However in 1960 articles began to appear in the local newspaper, that spoke of great interest in the Christian community of becoming unified . . . and being one in Christ.

These articles excited me, because of Nephi's prophecy, and I felt a strong impression to collect all the articles that I could and follow this "Unity" movement closely. Which I have done, since Dec 1960 to the present. This unity movement seems to be very important to the general world religious community; and has a web site on the Internet that reports progress on a regular basis, to the world. The movement also seems to be spear headed by the Catholic church, and is organized under the Ecumenical Council of that church (See "Christian Unity" on the Internet).

On Jan 6 1964 the Seattle Post Intelligencer ran an article, *"Pope OK's common bible translation. In cooperation with the separated Brethren, Protestant, Anglican, and Orthodox Christians as well. All Christians will be able to use them".* The unity movement has a common language. This effort alone removes a major stumbling block to "Christian Unity" and establishes a foundation for that effort.

Also on Nov 19, 1963, the Seattle Post Intelligencer ran an article quoting Billy Graham, the renowned evangelist, *"Graham predicts Vatican Council may Bring Christian Revolution".*

And on 6/27/11, I read on the Internet that the *"Maryland Episcopal Church will be the first in the US to join Roman Catholic Church".* This article also makes the point that the minister of this Episcopal Church will be able to continue in his ministry, with his flock.

On 9/12/11, I read on the Internet, *"More Anglicans to convert to Catholicism at Easter"*.

And in a Tacoma News paper dated Oct 28, 2011 there was an article describing an invitation made by Pope Benedict XVI, to Hindu's, Muslim's, Jews, and all Christian faiths worldwide. This invitation apparently met with good success. And all 300 invited faiths, came together and, lent their voices in individual prayers for peace.

One of my favorites . . . in the Tacoma News Tribune, dated May 8, 1999, *"Pope and Patriarch meet to heal nearly 1000 year old rift, to heal an old wound"* An old wound is healed. (see Rev. 13:3).

These are but a few of the articles I have collected, concerning Christian Unity, over the years.

I have no clue as to the name this coalition of Church's will give themselves, assuming they ever achieve unity, and I am sure that they don't either.

The Seattle paper, Post Intelligencer, in June 21, 1962, published an article on Christian Unity, and quoted the Vatican as follows:

"The different churches should consider themselves equally guilty of the separation: no church should presume to be the one true church of Christ. The future church resulting from the union of the present churches would not be identified with any existing church, but would be completely new".

As early as 1962 the Vatican established a premise that the name of the church coming out of the unity movement would be "completely new".

To my mind this published statement by the Vatican contains a "conclusionary thought" that unity may very well be achieved.

The principle motivation behind this great unity movement is the theme "Is Christ divided"? I can understand their concern. I believe their motivation to be honorable. They want peace from wars, and a cessation to such abominations as legalized abortions, legalization of homosexual marriages, rampant crime and drug use, dysfunctional families, and political greed and corruption that allows these things to flourish. I believe that they feel that if they are united, they can have a profound, and more influential effect on politicians, and societal mores. And they are probably right. Besides did not Paul advocate the unity of the Church in Ephesians 4:1-16?

I have listened to the views of Dr. Timothy Nolan one of the Catholic Cardinals of the USA, over the fox News channel, and I agree with his views and concerns for our society.

For 236 years Christianity has served our nation very well and helped to make it the most powerful nation on earth. However in the past several decades Christianity has failed our societies and today finds itself greatly diminished in attendance, finances and influence in the world. Perhaps it will come back.

Scenario #2

There exists in the world today unprecedented levels of greed and corruption. And nowhere is this more prevalent than in the political arena of our cultures worldwide. Many politicians have made a career out of living off the tax payers and do so for they own personal gain subordinating any allegiance to the electorate to their lust for wealth, power, and perks.

Many of these people espouse a principle of the day that has become increasingly prevalent in our society known as, *"the end justifies the means"*.

This principle is Satanic in nature, and was introduced to the world, in the 1800's by Karl Marx the father of an ideology known as socialism, or communism, or fascism. All three of these societal destroying philosophys, came from the brain of a man who considered religion . . . "the opiate of the masses".

Many politicians employ this principle and throw honesty, fair play, and virtue out the window, in their scramble for wealth at the expense of the taxpayers.

There may be exceptions to this report . . . but the majority appear to be career politicians.

I know that some of our politicians believe they can make a difference. But even these, to some extent, must play the game of "compromise".

The greed candidly displayed by politicians is contagious and prevails through out our society today.

Politicians are the top of the money and power food chain because they have the authority to spend taxpayer money.

I would have to suggest organized labor as next in line at the public trough. This group represents virtually every manufacturing, service, or distribution segment of our society. This group has as a basic principle . . . *"if you don't join, you don't work".* That sounds like *"the end justifies the means",* doesn't it.

A clear intent to exercise control over the agency of other people to ensure the power and wealth of people in charge.

Also the unions return much of the tax payer money, they receive, from politicians back to politicians, as contributions, in order to ensure "their favorite candidates" are re-elected. This money laundering process appears as a contribution and is therefore considered legal, and helps to keep the politician in power to continue to feed the power and money food chain.

The "God" of these groups is money and power. The power to control the lives of men so that their positions of wealth and power remain secure and unthreatened.

The next group on this food chain of wealth and power are certain segments of our society that have become funded money "sinks", for the express purpose of buying votes and obtaining contributions.

Some illustrations are as follows:

1. Man made global warming. Again a money laundering scheme. Certain companies who have contributed to candidates receive large contracts as a reward, and then continue to make contributions to the candidate.
2. Abortions to woman on demand at tax payer expense.
3. Birth control provisions given to women at tax payer expense.
4. Marriage of homosexuals to ensure fairness. (A mere sexual preference has become a cause celebrate)
5. The arts.
6. Peanut farmers, who continue to receive taxpayer subsidizes long after the need is gone.
7. Corn farmers to ensure availability of ethanol.
8. A Social security stipend. Monthly payments to retired senior citizens to ensure they don't go hungry. For some elderly this is the only income they have. This very large support program is considered an "entitlement". Meaning everyone gets the benefit when they reach the proper age and apply for it.
9. Medicare. Like Social Security this is also an entitlement in the field of health care.
10. Faith-Based partnerships with the 13 government agencies of the Obama Administration (See scenario 4).

These items ensure that the politicians stay in office to continue to fuel the flow of money. Rendering large segments of our society dependent on government.

And thus the loyalty of many citizens are bought and paid for by taxpayer dollars.

The prevailing principle of those in this "food chain", is of a necessity socialistic in nature. Almost all involved in this "food chain" are so rabid and determined that the status quo be carefully maintained that radio talk show hosts have referred to them . . . as "a religion".

This "food chain" is powerful and vigorously resists changes or even an interruption.

The glue that holds this consortium together is the media. The media has long since failed all journalistic standards, and has entered the realm of "agenda participant".

In the early days of our nation the founding Fathers, expected the news media to be the "prod" that kept the government in line. And so it has been for most of my lifetime. By keeping the public informed, of malfeasance in government office, the press, has kept the government in line. However over the past several decades it has changed until today, the majority of the press has become the propaganda arm of the Democratic Political Party. And has had great success in convincing the public to accept the, ever increasing, socialist agenda of that political party.

The media, with the exception of Fox News, is the bully pulpit that pounds the eardrums of the citizenry relentlessly and fulfills the age old premise, "tell a man a lie often enough and soon he'll accept it as a truth". And guess what? That actually works. Adolph Hitler, used this premise in his attempt, to establish fascism in Germany in the early 1900's . . . and it worked.

This scenario briefly describes the current "Great and Abominable Church" of materialism.

Scenario #3

At present there is a global influence in the world known as the United Nations. Most nations, certainly all-major nations, are members of this organization and support it with taxpayer money. This organization currently has a standing army. The United Nations original charter, when it was set up as the League of Nations many years ago, was envisioned as a world peacekeeper. But as in all cases, in this world of man, where there are large concentrations of money greed and corruption are not far behind. And the United Nations is no exception.

Recently Michael Medved, on his talk show, hosted a man by the name of Dick Morris. This man, Mr. Morris, is a political engineer, pollster, author and columnist. He has been closely involved with both political parties, for many years, and has a wealth of experience in the political arena. I have listened to him a number of times and am always interested in his political opinion. Mr. Morris has recently written a book entitled, "Here Come The Black Helicopters" by Dick Morris and Eileen McGann. Mr. Medved in his daily talk show (about 10/18/12) interviewed Mr. Morris and did a brief review of this recent book. In the books web site description it states the following as a lead in:

"Stealthily advancing the globalist and socialists at the UN, and within the USA itself, are trying to dilute our national sovereignty and undermine our democratic values and mandate massive transfers of our

wealth and technology to third world countries. They want to create a "global governance" where lasting and critical decisions are made by the UN and institutional commission, instead of by our elected officials".

Mr. Morris pointed out that he is of the opinion that Mr. Obama and other key democrats want to enter into treatise's that gives the UN world sovereignty. All treatise's entered into by the President of the USA must be ratified by the Congress. However with the help of the Senate leader, Mr. Harry Reid, and his quorum of "yes men", Mr. Obama has rendered the congress impotent; however, Mr. Barack Obama, can accomplish treatise approval by executive order. He has used the executive order process for the past 5 years, to advance his socialist agenda through onerous regulations that restrict and impede free enterprise.

I ask myself " is it inconceivable that any of our elected politicans would negotiate away this nation to the United Nations for a personal position of wealth and power, in a world organization, into perpetuity"? Also, how meaningful to the citizens of the United States is national sovereignty . . . in consideration of our love affair with European social life and judicial preferences?

Perhaps Mr Morris's thoughts are not to far fetched.

Scenario # 4

Faith-Based and Community Initiatives sponsored by the Federal Government could easily become what Nephi saw. This initiative set-up by President Bush in Jan 2001, was centered in the Department of Health and Human Services, and allegedly created opportunities for religions to interface with government agencies in a non-financial partnership. However in 2009 President Obama made some changes. He changed the name of this initiative to "White House Office of Faith-Based and Neighborhood Partnerships". Now the White House oversees faith-based centers in 13 government agencies, and makes their partners aware of "where to apply for grants". (See Deseret News dated May 19, 2013, page 6 on Faith-Based Initiatives)

Any religion that accepts money from the government will be managed by the government. Based on the above referenced news article the LDS Church prefers to "go it alone". This initiative on the part of the government literally blows away the separation of Church and State arguments and opens wide the potential for the literal fulfillment of what the Prophet Nephi saw come to past. Combine this scenario with number 3 and in a year or so we could have a unified Christianity, having been bought by the government, with a standing army as seen by the Apostle John.

This kind of "government-religion" partnership was practiced in the Roman Empire, between the 1st and the 4th centuries. The Roman Empire was very tolerant towards most religions, many arising out of the worship of Pagan Deities. The Romans set-up what could be called a federal agency, with the title, *"Pontifex Maximus"* to manage these religions. Any religion listed by this office was entitled to special consideration, even financial assistance. Religions not recognized were subject to extermination. Christianity, in the first and second century was not recognized by *Pontifex Maximus,* and was a persecuted religion, both by the Roman Government and the Jews. (See "Apostasy To Restoration" by T. Edgar Lyon, page 20).

This modern day government-religion partnership could easily become a "persecuting" government, showing favor to those who accept government grants and therefore government regulation and controls, and penalties to religions who "go-it-alone".

These scenarios are conspiracy theories on my part. However based on the shortness of time, I will go out on a limb here, and make the suggestion that *"those who have an eye to see and an ear to hear . . ."* will see signs appearing within the next two years and will recognize them as, the beginning of, the fulfillment of Nephi's prophecy.

I am certain that what Nephi saw, as a world power, was a church. Nephi was a prophet of God. Most certainly he knows what a church is. Also he compared it to the Church of the Lamb of God, when he said he saw "save two churches". And he most definitely knew the Church of the Lamb of God. So yes . . . he saw a time when there would be only two Churches.

But why a Church? Why would the organization that is prophesied to become the last world power, in the last days, represent itself as a church?

Think about it. The vast majority of people worldwide pay homage to a God. They want to believe in and worship a God. Such worship is natural and much more comfortable to people, worldwide. Churches suggest to the mind charity, benevolence, outreach, and concern. Churches tend to be associated with the kinder side of humanity. A well established religious organization is the most apt to capture the hearts and minds of man. Also the designation "Church" is more acceptable to the world than the term "Government". Governments, world wide, have become an enemy, and an impediment, to individual freedom and peace.

The existence of this "Church of the Devil", or Mega-Church, on the world scene is a very key event signaling that the events of the last days have become a reality.

Having said that who will it be? What scenario of the four is most likely? Only time will tell. I am confident that this last "World Dominating" entity is presently in place, in embryo, and all the key players are on the scene to bring it to the fore in our society. The governments will play their role and the churches theirs and the socialist of the world, the antichrist's of our day, will play their role. This last world ruler will begin to make its self visible late this year and very recognizable next.

One thing is sure as it emerges it will be hailed as a "Savior" of our society. Bringing calm, peace and sensibility to everyday life. In a short time it will be adored even worshipped.

It is only that kind of posture that can invoke a universal emotion in the society of man as deep and poignant as "worship". And it is this worship that gives this entity the authority to exercise world dominion.

The media will be the principle enthusiast in announcing the progress and extolling the greatness of this entity. It will emerge on the world scene as a "breath of fresh air".

Have I spoken prophetically? Some may think so . . . I do not. To me this is just common sense. I have "studied it out in my mind" (See D/C 9:7-9) prayerfully, and I can say . . . as Spock would say . . . "it is logical".

CHAPTER 11

APOLOGIST

I n these writings, of the "Last Days", I have made predictions that certain things would happen and result in specific consequences. I tried to document my assertions by references to applicable scripture; however, there are predictions that I have made that have no scriptural reference.

Some close friends have questioned if I felt I was speaking prophetically and therefore assuming to much. I had the same concerns. But I wrote as I felt impressed by the spirit . . . at least I felt that I did. And I had the distinct impression that I dared not deny what I have written.

This raises the question . . . do I have the right to speak/ write prophetically? A question that prompts this chapter.

Are their Prophets in the Church of Jesus Christ of Latter Day Saints other than those who lead and guide the Church? What are the qualifications of such a Prophet? How are they made manifest and are they true Prophets? How do they differ from the 1st Presidency and the Quorum of the Twelve?

In the bible, Numbers 11:29 Moses stated; *Enviest thou for my sake? Would God that all the Lords people were prophets, and that the Lord would put his spirit upon them*".

Moses would have liked to see all Israel, as a nation of prophets who had the Lords spirit.

Moses knew the same thing that John the Revelator declared in Revelations 19:10, . . . *"Worship God for the testimony of Jesus is the spirit of prophesy"*.

A testimony of Jesus only comes by the spirit of revelation . . . the Holy Ghost. In such a revelation a person, man or women (Miriam was a Prophetess), knows that Jesus is the Christ and that He lives, and is the source of grace unto salvation. This knowledge carries with it the spirit or inspiration of prophesy.

Why? Because the source of spiritual inspiration to mortal man is the Holy Ghost. The Holy Ghost is the spirit of revelation. He is the testifier of the Lord Jesus Christ and God the Father.

To one who loves the Lord Jesus Christ, and has complied with His "doctrine" the witness of the Holy Ghost is made manifest . . . in abundance.

Ancient Israel had many Prophets in addition to those whose writings are part of the old testament record. (See 1 Sam 10:5-11, 1 King 18:13, & 2 King 2:5).

And in Acts 2:17 we read, *"And it shall come to pass in the last days, saith God, I will pour out of my spirit upon all flesh: and your sons and your daughters shall prophesy, and your young men shall see visions, and your old men shall dream dreams"* (See Bible topical guide, Prophecy, page 396).

I know that leaders of the LDS Church, in the past, have made reference to the part of this revealed truth about ". . . *and your young men shall see visions, and your old men shall dream dreams"* . . . as reference to divine revelations that facilitated inventions and improvements in all walks of life and especially medical science. However, *"sons and daughters who prophesy"* is a matter that pertains to spiritual circumstances of the Church.

The word *"prophesy",* quoted above, in foot notes, makes reference to Acts 21:9 where we read *"And the same man had four daughters, virgins, which did prophesy".* On this occasion Paul, and his company, were visiting Caesarea and were in the home of Phillip the evangelist, *"and one of the seven",* who apparently had four daughters who prophesied. Also while Paul lingered with Phillip, their came a prophet, by the name of Agabus, who took Paul's girdle and wrapped it around his own hands and feet and prophesied to Paul that thus would he be bound by the Jews if he went to Jerusalem (See Acts 21:8-10). And so on this occasion in Paul's life, while visiting Phillip, he comes in contact with five prophets and recognizes them as such.

In 1 Corinthians 14:37 Paul declared, *"If any man think himself to be a prophet, or spiritual, let him acknowledge that the things that I write unto you are the commandments of the Lord".* Paul, who in his fourteenth year was lifted up to the third heaven (See 2 Corinthians 12:2-4); and saw and heard things unspeakable, in that redeeming experience, knew that his commandments were from the Lord. And any one who could testify to that truth could only do so through a testimony of the Lord.

Again in 1 Corinthians 14:39 Paul declared" *Wherefore, brethren, covet to prophesy, and forbid not to speak with tongues".* In short, immerse yourselves in the knowledge and testimony of the Lord and make manifest the spiritual gifts that come from that precious association.

Paul in Romans 12:6 declared, *"Having then gifts differing according to the grace that is given to us, whether prophecy, lets us prophesy according to the proportion of faith"*. In this statement Paul recognized that one of the gifts of the spirit, given to the saints, is the gift to *"prophesy"*, *"according to the proportion of faith"* they may have.

Apparently in ancient times and, during the meridian of time it would appear that other prophets flourished and were equally recognized by those who the Lord had called and set-apart.

The inspiration of the Holy Ghost is the spirit of prophesy. In John 16:13, speaking of the gifts of the Holy Ghost, we read . . . *"and he will shew you things to come"*.

It is never the intent of the Lord to keep His disciples in the dark. In this simple statement the Lord reveals to His followers that the Holy Ghost will reveal to them things pertaining to future events, and circumstances that have a bearing on their lives. What could be more natural for the Lord to do for a faithful follower? After all . . . *"if ye are prepared ye shall not fear"*.

This inspiration from the Holy Ghost, when sought in prayer, can pertain to near term events or to more distant future events. Many Latter Day Saints are more familiar with revelation that pertains to near term events for themselves and/or their families. Probably because that is where their interest lies.

In my case, I wanted to know about the events of the last days and, more specifically, the potential impact on me and my family and extended family as a result of these latter day events.

In examining the mission of the Holy Ghost I am led to ponder . . . why did I feel concern about the last days in the first place? Did the spirit put these thoughts in my head or is it just due to a naturally inquisitive nature?

I came from heaven with a natural propensity for . . . order. All my life I have loved order and organization. Some years ago I learned, from a sociologist group presentation, that I attended, that I am what is known as a "linear thinker". Someone who tends to think in terms of right angles, and parallel lines. Of rules of performance or expectations, such as procedures, guidelines, etc; as opposed to a "abstract thinker" who is comfortable in less restricting circumstances.

As I read these, "last days", scriptures the feeling came to me to be logical in putting events in a practical order of occurrence which I have done.

To illustrate. The book of revelations in chapters 8-11 describes the horrible destruction the world will experience that saves the more righteous and destroys all of the wicked. And then several chapters later, in revelations 15, John talks about the "Beast" who is permitted to make war against the saints for 3.5 years. When, in reality the "Beast" and all the wicked are destroyed in the plagues described in revelations 8-11. Therefore the "Beast" must make war on the saints before the plagues described in revelations 8-11 occur. And in D/C 29:8 we are told that the saints will exodus to the safety of Missouri before the apocalypse spoken of in revelations 8-11 is unleashed on the world; but logically the exodus of the saints must occur after the "Beast" has made war on the saints for 3.5 years.

Hence the logical or practical order of these events is; the "Beast" makes war against the saints then, when that is over, the saints will exodus to Missouri, then the Apocalypse will occur and destroy all of the wicked.

That is, as I believe, the true and proper sequence of these three events. I don't think that violates the scriptures as written;

nor does it indicate that I am writing prophetically. I believe it means that I am using common sense.

In modern revelation, in the D/C 42:65 we read *". . . for unto you it is given to know the mysteries of the kingdom, but unto the world it is not given to know them"*.

The faithful Latter Day Saint will be blessed to, have revelation consistent with his/her spiritual maturity, faith, and desire.

It is true that people of the world understand, in general terms, that an apocalypse is coming, and . . . even expect it, because of their belief in God. But they do not understand the particulars of these events.

Many believe that, "Last Days" disasters, will be no worse than what we have experienced in the recent past. For example Shepherd Smith, a news anchor on Fox News, reported on one occasion that the worst earthquake we have ever experienced is a 10 on the Richter Scale. And local governments or a combination of governments and charities have so far been able to render relief in all of the disasters we have experienced to date.

During the week 11/19/12, Fox News ran a one hour review on the "Last Days" focusing on the anticipated disaster, that many expected to occur, at the ending of the Mayan calendar on Dec 21, 2012.

This review paraded experts before the camera to testify about the last days. To my surprise some believe that our current world wide, disaster, experiences are the events referred to as the apocalypse in The Book of Revelations. How very naïve.

The Lord revealed, to the Prophet Joseph Smith, that the cataclysmic events of the last days would *"break down the mountains, and the valleys shall not be found".* Also that *"the great deep shall be driven back into the north countries, and the islands shall become one land".* And He continues *"and the earth shall be like as it was in the days before it was divided"* (See D/C 133:22-24). This reconfiguration of the earth speaks to the tectonic plates moving back to their original configuration.

This kind of earth movement, that will happen in a very short time during the apocalypse; will be so violent it will cause the earth to *"reel to and fro like a drunken man"* (See Isaiah 24:20, D/C 49:23 and D/C 88:87).

These scriptures speak to unprecedented destruction as this reconfiguration of the earth takes place. The earthquakes will literally knock the stylist off the Richter Scale. The governments of the world will be rendered completely impotent. All surviving peoples will be isolated. Just think about that. No radio, no TV, no town or city help, no cell phones. The roads so broken up not even a jeep vehicle can traverse them. Houses so damaged that the only shelter they provide is similar to a cave, with no amenities.

This kind of thing has happened before. At the crucifixion of the Lord the Nephites experienced physical damage to the earth so severe that the survivors were isolated by a complete vapor of darkness for three days (See 3 Nephi 8:20-23).

Have current day disasters caused the world to repent? Absolutely not. In fact church attendance has declined in the Christian world. To their credit the world has rushed to the aid of those experiencing disasters. And yes many have rightly concluded that these disasters are a call to repentance. Nevertheless these disasters have not produced a change in societal behavior. Ergo . . . current disasters are not the anticipated catastrophic experience! Why? Because the Lords prophesied destruction will produce change in peoples behavior. Which contemporary disasters have failed to do.

Am I being prophetic in these last several paragraphs or just being practical and using common sense?

There are no limitations to the "mysteries of God". The Lord told us *"Ask and it shall be given you. Seek and ye shall find; knock and it shall be opened unto you"* (Matt 7:7). The only limiting factor in our association with our God is . . . us.

We mortals tend to build a hypothetical box around ourselves, based on our knowns and unknowns, our experiences and our lack of experience. Things we take ownership of and things we consider out of our range of expertise. This hypothetical box is our comfort zone.

We do this to ourselves because we really don't like circumstances that make us uncomfortable or cause us to feel diminished or exposed in any way.

Such a growth restriction is completely incongruent with the concept of progress. If we are ever to become better than we are we must learn to think out-side of our box.

All faithful members of the Church of Jesus Christ of Latter Day saints, who hold and honor temple recommends and have a strong and binding testimony of the Lord Jesus Christ, are entitled to the "spirit of prophesy". And if they feel so impressed they too can and should exercise this gift and blessing.

In point of fact one of the spiritual gifts promised to the saints is the gift of Prophecy. In D/C 46:22, we read *"And to others it is given to prophesy"*. In this revelation, given to the Prophet Joseph Smith, March 8, 1831, the Lord enumerates the gifts of the spirit. And this verse speaks specifically to the gift of prophesy. Verses 10 through 30, of this chapter, are devoted to an enumeration, by the Lord, of spiritual gifts that faithful saints can experience. And in verse 26 the Lord declares, *"And all these gifts come from God, for the benefit of the children of God"*. Apparently any who experience these gifts are expected to use them for the benefit of the *children of God.*

Could members, of the Church, prophesy for the Church? No! In fact there is an old adage in the church that says . . . "never get ahead of the Prophet".

However can lay-members of the church prophesy for themselves or families about events and or circumstances that could effect them in their individual lives or as members of the church? I believe so. When moved upon by the Holy Ghost. For example see Paul's experience quoted above with a prophet named *"Agabus"* who prophesied for an apostle of the church.

Also what did the *"sons of the prophets"* tell Elisha, the understudy of Elijah, as the time for the departure of Elijah came close? They said to Elisha, *"Knowest thou that the Lord will take away thy master from thy head this day?"* And Elisha answered, *"Yea, I know it; hold ye your peace"* (See 2 Kings 2:5).

Here is an account of a group of prophets who prophesied to Elisha the understudy of the renowned Elijah. What was different about this group of *"sons of the prophets"* and Elisha or Elijah? The answer to that question is "the mantle of the Lord". How so?

What Elisha feared happened. Elijah was indeed taken up into heaven *"in a chariot of fire"*.

Elisha was terribly distraught at this happening and cried *"My Father, my Father"* and rent his clothes. And as Elijah was carried into heaven his mantle fell from his shoulders and Elisha picked it up. Elisha took the mantle and smote the waters of a river, as he had seen Elijah do, and the waters divided and he crossed over. Now *"50 of the sons of the prophets"* had witnessed the whole thing and when they saw how Elisha used Elijah's mantle they said, *"The spirit of Elijah doth rest on Elisha. And they came to meet him and bowed themselves to the ground before him"* (See 2 King 2:5-15). They recognized the power and the authority of the "mantle".

Today we recognize the mantle of the Lord on our Leaders. The mantle represents "one chosen by the Lord" and carries with it the keys of the priesthood that are necessary for that leader to fulfill his calling. Further more our leaders are called by one having authority, hands are laid on their heads to delegate keys, and, instead of bowing before these leaders, we raise the right hand in a sustaining vote. Do they have "the spirit of prophesy"? Oh! Most definitely. Bishops, and Stake Presidents, are "common judges in Israel". As judges, by assignment of keys, they have the spirit of revelation, to provide guidance and direction in the lives of the saints. And we sustain the Presidency of the Church and the quorum of the twelve as Prophets, Seers and Revelators.

Also obedience on the part of members to the counsel of our leaders who hold keys of the Priesthood have the promise *"of the more sure word of prophesy"* (See 2 Peter 1:19), in their lives. In short if they follow the council of the sustained prophets they have the promise, through faith, of experiencing the blessings promised by the counsel.

On the other hand Saints who prophesy, *"according to the proportion of their faith"* (See Romans 12:6 above), receive no keys, were not called and are not sustained to function as the Lords anointed in His Church. The only "mantle" they have *". . . are the gifts according to the grace that is given to them . . . according to the proportion of their faith"*. Nevertheless their prophesies are just as true as those who hold keys, because their thoughts also come from the source of all truth, . . . the Holy Ghost. And the Holy Ghost will never, never cause a lay member of the Church to "get ahead of a prophet who wears the mantel of the Lord".

Now lets reason together. The purpose of the "last days" is to separate the righteous from the wicked and remove the wicked from this earth and complete the "Restoration" of all things.

The scriptures tell us this separation will begin on the Lords house first and then the world. Those who survive do so because they are entitled to live in a terrestrial estate as judged by the Lord. A terrestrial estate is unquestionably a much more joyous life than the telestial estate . . . the one we now live in.

The only thing in question, in all of this "last days" discussion . . . is timing. If you take Johns revelation chapter eight verse one literally then everything I have written makes sense. And Elder Boyd K Packer of the quorum of the 12 apostles has said *"trust the scriptures"*.

One thing is absolutely certain no matter what you choose to believe relative to the "last days". If you want to be saved and live in a terrestrial world . . . <u>you must follow the counsel of our sustained priesthood leaders faithfully.</u>

Now what is "common sense" to me may be "prophetic" to someone else who hasn't taken the time to think it through. People of my own family have said *"I am not going to worry about such things, I will trust in God"*. There is absolutely nothing wrong with preferring to remain uninformed about the details of the "last days". The "last days" will occur whether we think about them or not. I simply wanted to know more about them.

Every faithful member of the Church has access to the spirit of all truth, based on their faith, their desire, and the effort they make . . . to know. And that thought is very key to experiences of inspiration.

What did the Lord tell Oliver Cowdery when he sought the gift to translate? In D/C 9:7-9, Oliver Cowdery was instructed that in order to receive inspiration one must study it out in his mind and reach a conclusion, and then appeal to the Lord to learn if it is correct. And the Lord promises that if it is not correct the applicant will receive a stupor of thought and if it is correct he will receive a burning in his bosom.

My dear friends . . . I have had no stupor of thought. If anything the urgency and intensity of interest in this book has been a very, very . . . lively experience.

In these last days, I believe that, what Moses hoped for has come to pass; for all, baptized members of the LDS Church who have a testimony that Jesus is the Christ have the spirit of prophesy (Rev. 19:10).

CHAPTER 12

TIME ANALYSIS

I wrote this chapter to explain my thoughts on timing as it pertains to the events of the "last days".

This term, "last days" is used primarily by Christians who have respect for the beliefs and teachings of the Lord Jesus Christ. And the term makes reference to prophesied events associated with the second coming of Christ.

Through the ages Prophets have, with joy, looked forward to the second coming of the Lord in the last days. A time when the world will enter a condition that can only be described as Utopia. A time free of pain, sorrow, evil, sickness and even death. A time described as the millennium reign of the Lord Jesus Christ, who will reign in person on planet earth.

However the scriptures make the point that before this Utopia comes the earth is to be cleansed of all wickedness.

History teaches that God, in one way or another, has been closely watching over man for a period of time totaling

6000 years before the year 2000. This time frame is as follows:

From Adam to the Meridian of time.   Zero to 4000 BC;
equals 4000 years.

From the Meridian of time to modern man. Zero to 1999 AD
equals 2000 years.

Total   6000 years.

(For chronology see "The wall chart of world history, by Edward Hull,
The, Chronology of the KJV Bible pg 636-645, and Internet Bible World
History Timeline)

This total period of 6000 years represents 6 Millennia. The year 2000 is the beginning of the next one-thousand year period of time in which the Millennial reign, the restoration of all things, is to occur. And at the time of this writing we are presently twelve years, and a little bit, into the 7th thousand year period of time.

I know that "no one not even the angels" know the time of the second coming of the Lord Jesus Christ (see Matthew 24:36).

But when will the cleansing of the earth begin in preparation for the second coming of the Lord?

Looking up the term "Last Days", in my CD on scriptures, I found over 260 scriptures that talk to "last day" themes. These themes, generally speaking, make reference to such events as "the gathering of Israel", "the redemption of Israel", "Lords house to be established in the top of the mountains", "earth to be at war", even a reference to the war Michael will fight at the end of the millennium. And many references to the covenants the Lord will establish with the house of Israel. But not one word about timing other than the general reference . . . "last days or latter days".

In the New Testament, Matthew chapter 24 speaks of the days of "tribulation" and second John, speaks of Anti-Christ's in the last days, and perilous times that will come, and that the saints will be persecuted and the book of revelations describes two prophets who will defend Jerusalem from the hoards and, of course almost the entire book of revelations is devoted to the "Last Days".

The Book of Mormon speaks of enduring to the end, that Israel is to be gathered, . . . only the obedient are to be saved, and the world is to be burned by fire.

It also makes reference to the Lord showing tender mercies to the Lamanites in the last days.

And 3 Nephi speaks to the terrible role of the "Sons of Jacob", and the eventual triumph of Israel.

The Doctrine and Covenants reveals that Independence, Missouri is the place for the New Jerusalem and the Temple of the Lord.

The Doctrine and Covenants also declares that the servants of the Lord are to "proclaim the abomination of desolation of the last days" (D/C 84:111-120). In this scripture latter-day-saints are instructed to *"Proclaim the abomination of desolation of the last days",* to the world. Or, in other words, proclaim to the world that unless they repent of abominations, the Lord will make it desolate (See Dan 11:31).

D/C 86:5, tells us that the angels are crying day and night to "reap down the fields".

D/C 109, "Judgment is to be poured out without measure".

D/C 113, speaks to the "gathering of my people" and "priesthood to have a great role in the last days"

So the scriptures tell us a great deal about the last days but no mention of timing.

Hyrum M Smith a former apostle of the church and co-author Janne Sjodahl, in their book Doctrine & Covenants Commentary, page 816, in reference to D/C 130: 14-17 (see note 2 below), makes two points concerning the second coming of the Lord.

1. The early disciples asked the *"Lord when he would come and what the signs of his coming would be"?*
   (See Matt 24:3, Mark 13:4, and Luke 21:7). And His answer revealed many things that would come to past, and signs that would be given but not one word about . . . when.
2. In D/C 130:14 We read of the earnest prayer of the Prophet Joseph Smith to know *"the time of the coming of the Son of Man".* However in reading verse 15, we see that the Lord had *"no intention of satisfying Joseph's curiosity".* In fact the Prophet was admonished *"trouble me no more on this matter".*

Those who are baptized members of the church are promised that the Holy Ghost *"will show them things to come"* (See John 16:13). I interpret this to mean that the Holy Ghost will give baptized members of the Lords church, . . . an understanding of events that are as yet futuristic. That is, of course, assuming that they are worthy, and want to know and make the effort to know.

So where does one start on this journey to learn about the timing of future events? Or does such "timing revelations" even exist?

It is common knowledge throughout Christendom that the Book of Revelations is a compilation of scripture, that in the main are, specifically designed to speak to the "last days". To the average Christian this book is hard to read and harder to understand. How credible is it and is it worth the effort to try and learn from it?

We learn from the Book of Mormon, that the Prophet Nephi, who saw every futuristic thing that John the revelator did was <u>not</u> permitted to write them. *"And behold, the things which this apostle of the Lamb shall write are many things which thou hast seen; and behold, the remainder shalt thou see. But the things which thou shalt see hear after thou shalt not write; for the Lord God hath ordained the apostle of the Lamb of God that he should write them".* (See Nephi 14:24-25).

And then Nephi names this apostle of the Lamb of God. *"And I, Nephi, heard and bear record that the name of the apostle of the Lamb was John, according to the word of the angel"* (See Nephi 14:27).

John the apostle and John the Revelator are the same person as the Apostle that Nephi has reference to. And he is the only one of all the prophets of the Lord, that had the assignment to record the specifics of timing, and details pertinent to the last days.

Apparently even the Lord in His dealings with His disciples in the Meridian of time and later with the Prophet Joseph Smith in the Dispensation of the Fullness of Times, honored the assignment of John; as his assignment relates to revealing a more in-depth explanation of the last days.

In fact the Lord saw to it that John, His beloved, was not killed as the other members of the original quorum of twelve, but was exiled to a penal colony on the Isle of Patmos, where he had the privilege of fulfilling his assignment of writing the Book of Revelations, . . . a record of a Jew. John being the Jew.

Of the Book of Revelation to be written by John; Nephi said: "*. . . the things which he shall write are just and true . . .* "Keep in mind that Nephi is also a prophetic witness to everything that John saw and recorded. Not only did Nephi see these things that John wrote of but so did Lehi, Nephi's Father.

Nephi bears a strong testimony of John's writings, . . . *and behold they are written in the book which . . . proceeded out of the mouth of a Jew".* Nephi makes it clear that John's record is a record of Gods dealings with the Jews. "*And . . . at the time these things proceeded out of the mouth of a Jew, the things that were written were plain and pure, and most precious, and easy to the understanding of all men"* (see 1 Nephi 14: 23).

Nephi bears record to the "*plainness, the purity and the preciousness"* of John's record, when . . . it "*proceeded out of the mouth of the Jew".*

Most people who read the Book of Revelations can bear testimony that it is anything but plain . . . apparently because of what the King James scholars did to the plainness . . . right?

Wrong! Joseph Smith who read the same Book of Revelations that we read said . . . "*The Book of Revelations is one of the plainest books God ever caused to be written"* (See Church History 5th volume, page 342).

Perhaps if we enjoyed the close association of the Holy Ghost that a Prophet of the Lord does, the Book of Revelations would be plain and precious to us, as well. So I guess we have to work a little harder at understanding.

The Book of Revelations is what it is. It is the record that an omnipotent God has seen fit to survive the passage of time and pass down through the ages, . . . since its pure inception . . . past the uninspired scholars of King James, and into the hands of you and I, in these last days, to come forth "*as one of the plainest books God ever caused to be written*".

Hence it is more than adequate to be a source of guidance to us. We are, in point of fact, as accountable to the information contained in the Book of Revelations as we are to any of the canon of scripture. And the Holy Ghost who will "*show us things to come*", will give us guidance in understanding this plain and precious record of a Jew.

Now back to the point of our study. Does the Book of Revelations reveal to you and I the timing of the beginning of the preparation of the earth for the second coming of the Lord? The answer to this question is . . . yes! Most of the timing referenced in this book describes how long a specific event will last. Such as a 5 month war, or the 3.5 years that 2 prophets protect Jerusalem, and so forth.

However there is only one scripture that I have found, in the book of revelations, that makes reference to the beginning of the apocalypse of the Last Days.

I have explained this scripture in chapter 8, the chapter I tried to publish as a, stand alone writing to several newspapers. For continuity in this chapter I will repeat the method once again however in a little more detail, as this chapter does pertain to "timing".

Revelations 8:1 says:

"*And when he had opened the seventh seal, there was silence in heaven about the space of half an hour.*

The "He" in this scripture is the Lord. In the previous chapters 6 & 7, of the Book of Revelations, we read of the opening of six seals by the Lord. So now, in chapter 8, the Lord opens the 7th seal. Each seal represents a millennium of the earth. As you can see from the timing at the beginning of this writing the six millennia take us through the year 1999. The next year, . . . the year 2000, . . . is the beginning of the 7000th period of time, of Gods dealings with man and begins the 7th millennia that "modern man" has been on earth.

In D/C 77:12 the Prophet Joseph Smith speaking of Rev. 8, says ". . . and the sounding of the trumpets of the seven angels are the preparing and finishing of his work, in the beginning of the seventh thousand years—the preparing of the way before the time of his coming".

According to the Prophet Joseph Smith "the preparing and the finishing of the Lords work" . . . are to occur in the "beginning of the seventh thousand years" . . . in the beginning of the year 2000, "before the time of His coming". Its clear to me that the Prophet Joseph Smith knew the approximate time of the preparing of the earth for the coming of the Lord. It would start and be finished in the beginning of the seventh thousand year. And as I write we are already 12 years, and a little bit, into the seventh thousand year period.

I must confess I have no idea how long "beginning" is in terms of time. I would suggest that 2013 is 13 years into the beginning of the 7,000th year and a very good beginning, and yet . . . nothing yet. So obviously the term "beginning" is longer than 13 years. But I have a feeling it is not much longer.

So when the Lord opened this 7th seal and initiated the 7,000th year, John records that there is to be . . . *silence in* heaven about the space of half an hour". This word "about" is a conundrum. It means "approximately" and can be interrupted as either plus or minus relative to the prophesied time of half an hour.

What about the phrase," *silence in heaven';* what does that mean? The term "silence" means . . . *"stillness, quietness, calm, or mute".* I take this to mean that during this one-half hour, Heaven will exercise no more influence upon man, than is currently being experienced. However the ominous suggestion is that after that one-half hour their will no longer be . . . *silence in heaven.*

Apparently after this half-hour, as the 8th chapter of revelations continues and on through chapter 11 . . . the apocalypse breaks out on the earth with a vengeance.

So then what reckoning are we to use in defining this one-half hour? If it means mans time then it defies understanding as many one-half hour periods of time have come and gone since the beginning of the year 2000, and nothing has happened . . . no apocalypse.

However if this is the Lords time that is an entirely different matter. Now what is one-half hour of the Lords time? Peter in 2 Peter 3:8 declares, *But, beloved be not ignorant of this one thing, that one day is with the Lord as a thousand years, and a thousand years as one day".*

So there we have it . . . the reckoning of the Lord defined by Peter. One of His days is equivalent to one thousand of our years. So then lets divide the Lords day of one thousand of our years by 24, . . . and we find one of the Lords hours is 41.66 of our years. What then is one-half an hour? Divide 41.66 by 2 and we get 20.833. Lets round that up to 21 for ease of handling. Now add 21 to the year 2000 and we come up with 2021. This is the year when the cleansing of the earth could begin. (See the book "The Millennial Messiah", by Elder Bruce R McConkie, page 382).

Assuming the year 2021 to be the year the apocalypse commences then many events must transpire before that day. The D/C 29:8 refers to the apocalypse as days of "tribulation and desolation".

The word "tribulation" means unprecedented damage and the word "desolation" means to depopulate. Scary terms. But this verse says that the faithful saints will be *"gathered into one place upon the face of the land . . . and be prepared against tribulation and desolation".*

Apparently the saints will be in a safe and protected place before the apocalypse will begin.

But when will they move to this place of protection and what will cause them to go there?

Through out millennia the prophets have spoken of the persecution that will befall the covenant people of the Lord in the "last days". In fact the persecution of the meridian-of-days-saints is a shadow of what will happen to the latter-day-saints.

Before the saints will exodus to "a safe place" interesting things are going to happen in the world that will directly effect the saints.

It would appear that at a time . . . *"yet to be determined"*, the entity known as the "Beast" will make war with the saints for 42 months. If the saints exodus the world in 2021 then the 42 month war the beast will initiate on the saints must begin, at the latest, 42 (Rev.13:5-8) months earlier or about June of 2017.

Why wouldn't the 'Beast" make war with the saints after they have moved into Jackson County, Missouri? Because when the saints are in Missouri they will be under the protection of the Lord and the "Beast" will fear the saints (See D/C 45:70). No the "Beast" will only have access to the saints while they are in the world.

I submit that the saints will one day, at a time . . . *yet to be determined,* be instructed by priesthood leadership on exactly what action to take, and it will involve the living of the law of consecration and leaving the society of the world; because of the saints refusal to join with the "Beast".

The *"Church of the lamb of God",* will be forced into an exodus, . . . an exodus that will, eventually, save it from the days of "tribulation and desolation", and save many faithful saints from the "Beast".

The apostle, John, also included specific time frames relative to the actual events of the apocalypse. For example:

Rev 9:5-10, speaks of a 5 month war.
Rev 9:15, speaks of angels from the pit who will slay man for 13 months.
Rev 11:2, speaks of the Holy City (Jerusalem) being trod under foot 3.5 years.
Rev 11:3, Two of the Lords witnesses will prophesy for a period of 3.5 years.

The Apostle John who had the assignment, of the Lord, to write the specifics about the apocalypse did indeed include time frames in his account, and even quantifies the extent of destruction that will occur.

Adding up the time frames in John's account we see that the "Beast" will make war against the Saints for 3.5 years. Then the saints and "others", those who the Lord will save", will be removed to Missouri.

The ensuing apocalypse will last about 12 years.

I count 3.5 years for the Tribulation phase and 8.3 years for the desolation years, for a total of 11.8 years. Then afterward the final event is a global conflagration.

The process of the apocalypse will also reconfigure the earth to its Paradisiacal Glory (see Rev 21:1 & Article of Faith #10). And then I anticipate that the Lord will come and bring the New Jerusalem with Him (See Rev 21:2).

It may all start 2021 for the world. . . . and much sooner for the saints . . . (see D/C 112:25-26).

However, *"If ye are prepared ye shall not fear".*

CHAPTER 13

THE AGENCY OF MAN

This subject is perhaps the most talked about subject in all of the revealed word of God. At the very center of agency is our choice between good or evil. Our agency is the entire point of our being in mortality in the first place. In point of fact the burden of the scriptures is to guide us to make correct choices in mortality through the righteous use of our agency.

This subject and our understanding of it has a direct bearing on whether or not we survive the apocalypse.

In the beginning . . .

After this earth was created it was the Fathers plan to send us, His spirit off-spring, to this earth to be tested and to prove ourselves all on our own. God knew we would sin and asked "who shall I send as the redeemer and savior of man kind"? Lucifer one of the sons of God didn't like Heavenly Fathers plan and wanted a risk free mortality. He offered a plan that would have taken agency from man and forced them to obey. Another son, whose name was Jehovah, stood up and offered a plan that would give us our agency and He would give His life for us, as an atonement, if necessary and bring back to the Father those, of us, who choose to be obedient.

Lucifer's plan was rejected, and he and his host rebelled against God. That's the short version of the "War in Heaven".

This rebellion was seen by the Apostle John who reported, *And their was war in heaven: Michael and his angels fought against the dragon; and the dragon fought and his angels, and prevailed not; neither was their place found anymore in heaven. And the great dragon was cast out, that old serpent, called the Devil, and Satan, which deceiveth the whole world: he was cast out into the earth and his angels were cast out with him".* (See Revelations 12:7-9)

(Note: By using this scripture I have introduced the name "Michael". Many christians are familiar with this name as "Michael the Arch-Angel"; and so he is. However in his mortal role he is known as "Adam"; the very valient, mortal head and Father of the entire human family who unquestionably earned this exalted role by virtue of his valiency . . . *in the first place).*

So for his rebellion, in the very presence of God, Lucifer was cast out of heaven along with his followers and earned the titles "Satan and Devil".

Obviously in our spirit life, in the pre-existence, we had agency and we had the ability to choose for our selves. This is evident in that Satan and his followers . . . fully one-third of all the billions of the hosts of Heaven rebelled against God (See D/C 29:36). One can't rebel if one doesn't have agency . . . can one? And isn't it interesting that Satan used the very agency he would have denied us to rebel against God.

So where did Satan and his hosts go?

Again John tells us . . . *"Woe to the inhabiters of the earth and of the sea! For the Devil is come down unto you having great wrath, because he knoweth that he hath but a short time"* (See Revelations 12:12)

So we have a very angry Satan somewhere on earth . . . if one believes the scriptures. Satan is a spirit. He was cast out of heaven and denied a body.

In fact many of his host wanted bodies so bad they were willing to take the bodies of swine as we learn from the Lords encounter with two wild man in the country of the Gergesenes (See Matthew 8:28-33).

But even the swine didn't want to be possessed by the devils and drowned themselves in the sea.

So where is Satan to day. He is all around us in the form of antichrists. Again as John told us in 1 John 2:22, *"Who is a liar but he that denieth that Jesus is the Christ? He is antichrist, that denieth the Father and the Son"*.

Where are the antichrists

Lets not confuse antichrists with disobedience to Gods commandments. They are not the same because of the principle of repentance. An antichrist rebels against Gods commandments and has no intent to repent . . . as Christ has commanded. These are mortals who may assume the appearance of being Christlike but are actually, openly or secretly, opposed to Christ (see Antichrist, KJV Bible dictionary pg. 609). In my life time I have been touched and impacted by antichrist.

My education, at the University of Utah, was interrupted by the Korean War that brought the draft board to my doorstep. Rather than go into the army for 90 days boot camp and then to Korea, I elected to join the Air Force and eventually was assigned in jolly old England.

In England I learned about communists. I had never heard of them. I learned they were the reason I was in the military in the first place.

I wanted to know more about them, and in the military that was easy to find out.

Satan who was rejected from Heaven, and cast down to the earth, had met up with a man by the name of Karl Marx. Mr. Marx and his friend Frederick Engle's wrote a book called the "Communist Manifesto" that clearly set them forth as socialist reformers and revolutionaries. Marx's position on religion was clear, he considered the worship of God "the opiate of the masses". To my thinking Marx's position on religion clearly indicates his source of inspiration. He also espoused another philosophy that to my thinking is criminal in nature; "the end justifies the means". This philosophy has no regard for my property or . . . my life for that matter. Therefore no regard for my agency.

Russia, China, Venezuela, North Korea, Cuba . . . nations that practice this philosophy are virtual slave nations. The citizens of these countries have no real agency they are subservient to the state for the wealth, comfort and perks of a ruling militant minority.

Apparently through the brain of Karl Marx Satan has achieved considerable success in establishing his original intent to control the agency of man on earth, in defiance of God.

The forerunner or the preparation of society for communism is socialism. Hence socialism, and communism are all peas in the same pod; with the common goal . . . the control of our agency.

Through the years unions have also distinguished themselves for the same practices and techniques as any well established socialistic society. Have you ever heard of the union closed shop? This stipulates that if you don't join you don't work. Again control of your agency.

For socialists, control of the agency of society is important in order to take their money as taxes and fees and give it to companies, groups or individuals who participate in the money laundering (payback) scheme to keep the political elitest wealthy and in power.

This kind of financial behavior is designed to build a large government to keep a political minority in power into perpetuity and creates two economic classes . . . the wealthy and the poor. The net effect of this action is to penalize individual self- reliance or initiative; and in that way control or manipulate the agency of the average man. Most probably the entire middle class . . . the largest economic class in America. Such behavior is selfish, and satanic in nature, and the exact opposite of the Lords plan for the people of this nation as provided for in the Constitution of the USA.

Gods plan for the agency of man

Gods plan for our agency is best illustrated in the law of the land . . . the constitution of the USA.

The constitution advocates the free agency of man, and is designed by God, through inspiration to the framers, to reward "self reliance". This principle guarantees us with the freedoms we need to provide for ourselves, not only the necessities of life, but even palatial living if that's what we want and can achieve.

Modern revelation, to The Church of Jesus Christ of Latter-Day-Saints, teaches that the Lord was instrumental in all circumstances concerning the framing, and creation of the Constitution of the United States of America. A review of the scriptures, surrounding this most momentous event, is both revealing, instructional, and . . . alarming.

D/C 98:6 reads, *"Therefore I the Lord, justify you, and your Brethren of my church, in befriending that law which is the constitutional law of the land";* . . .

Here the Lord makes it very clear to the LDS Church that He endorses the constitution of the USA and encourages the members of His Church to embrace the constitution.

In D/C 101:77, the Lord declared *"According to the laws and constitution of the people, which I have suffered to be established, and should be maintained for the rights and protection of all flesh, according to just and holy principles".*

In the early days of the LDS Church we were a persecuted faith. We experienced murders, rapes, confiscation of property, burning of our homes, destruction of our presses, and the murder of our leaders by mobs. The saints were driven out of the civilized society of the USA, in the middle of winter, into the frontier wilderness to perish.

Previous to the revelation quoted above The Lord had instructed the Prophet Joseph Smith to seek for redress, for persecutions against the saints by local governments, according to the laws of the constitution which the Lord established. The Lord then reveals that the constitution is based on *"just and holy principles".* Not only are the principles of the constitution "just" but they are "holy" as well. Who could possibly ask for more as a guide for the government of man? The Lord also counsels that the principles of the constitution are to *"be maintained for the rights and protection of all flesh".* It would seem that the Lord is here instructing this nation to be the world advocate for human rights and freedom for . . . all flesh not just America.

Doesn't it stand to reason that if God would stipulate that America assume the role of world protector that God would make America equal to that task?

In D/C 101:78, the Lord makes it clear that the reason He established the constitution is to establish an environment for the exercise of free agency in order that every man may be accountable for his own sins in the day of judgment. As the Lord declares in verse 79, *"Therefore it is not right that any man should be in bondage one to another"*.

The persecution of the saints, encouraged, by local and national political leadership in the 1830's was the same as putting the saints in bondage. And a man in bondage does not have the right of free exercise of his conscience. And of course this same divine counsel pertains to the principle of slavery being practiced at that time in the United States.

And in D/C 101:80, the Lord declares," *And for this purpose have I established the constitution of this land, by the hand of wise men whom I raised up unto this very purpose, and redeemed the land by the shedding of blood"*.

The Lord established the constitution for the express purpose of preventing any man from being brought into bondage, and He did it by "wise men . . . that He raised up for the very purpose of creating the constitution".

The phrase *"redeemed the land by the shedding of blood"*, has reference to the great Revolutionary War that, did indeed, see the shedding of much blood by the citizens of the new nation to earn their freedom from Great Britain.

To read these scriptures is to understand that God is the author of the constitution of the USA that it was prepared by men who He especially prepared, and raised up *"to that very purpose"*. And so by inference . . . anyone who seeks to circumvent the purpose and intent of this document is not inspired by the Lord, and finds themselves in opposition to Gods will.

The constitution is unique to the United States of America. A land that the Lord revealed in the Book of Mormon in 1 Nephi 2:20 as *"a land choice above all other lands"*.

There is no land anywhere in the world as choice as the land known as North America.

Based on the above quoted scriptures the Lord makes the point that He established the principles by which the United States is to be governed. However since the Lord loves all of His children we must also conclude that, in all probability, the Lord assisted other great nations in the initial framing of their laws pertaining to the establishment of governments and the duties of these governments to protect the rights of the citizens. More particularly those nations who guarantee the liberty and freedoms of its citizens.

And what has the constitution done for the United States of America?

The constitution has guided the USA to become the most powerful and influential nation in the world for 236 years. Indeed this nation has become the caretaker of the world. A nation that has pursued equal rights for all men and women in the world. A nation that has conquered many times, to depose tyrannical dictators, but has always returned the "conquered" land to the original inhabitants and helped the defeated to re-establish a government-by-the-people and restore its society, with all applicable infrastructure.

I personally am very proud of the role the USA has played in the world in my life time and rejoice in my citizenship.

The socialist in our nation are ashamed of the USA and feel that we have overplayed our hand in the world and should take a more benign role on the world scene.

Socialism on the other hand fails every time. Just look at the countries that are avid socialists such as Greece, Spain, Portugal and those mentioned above. Look also at the heavily socialist states in our nation and you will see similar failures.

All my adult life I have used the constitution as a guide to determine who I would vote for. Political candidates who supported the constitution got my vote. And for many years it seemed to me that most citizens of the United States were like minded. And then in Nov 2008 that all changed.

What have we done?

On Nov 2008 this nation voted for a man as the President of the USA that I know to be a Marxists. Marxists advocate the control of all manufacturing and distribution services of a nation. Marxism advocates a large bureaucratic government that can control the lives of the individuals, by making them dependant on the government for basic lifes needs.

This "Marxist government" is the exact opposite of government under the constitution. It requires heavy regulation and controls . . . all of which takes away liberty and as a consequence "agency".

Through Karl Marx, Satan has been enabled to establish his plan on earth that was originally vanquished in heaven, and the fight over that evil plan continues on earth . . . today. It is here . . . now . . . and has many supporters. Marxism is always recognizable in that it seeks to take away the agency of man.

This "Marxist" philosophy of government is currently practiced by many nations, in Europe, Asia, and South America, and those political experiments are all failing. In 20-40 years those nations who practice Marxism fail while the United States under the constitution was successful for 236 years. This failure of Marxism has been proven time after time and is a matter of history.

Then to add insult to injury the majority of citizens, in our nation on Nov. 6, 2012, voted this same Marxist President into power for a second four year term.

What are the consequences?

I believe that people today have lost sight of the constitution, and its purpose, and the great success it has brought our nation.

However there are consequences for rejecting Gods plan for Satan's plan. God described these consequences in the scriptures when He stated *"When the wicked rule the people mourn"* (See Proverbs 29:2 and D/C 98:9). I have a feeling that some of us may feel the "heel, of socialism, on our neck" sometime soon.

Our behavior has also informed our God that we as a nation no longer care about His constitution, and we want to experiment with a Marxist form of government.

History has proven, as long as we followed the Lords commandments he will fight our battles. History has also proven that nations who have rejected Gods will were shortly brought into the depths of humility, by adversity.

This elected President makes no bones that he does not support the constitution. In fact he has made it very clear that he wants to move our nation in the same direction as those failed Marxists nations. This could mean the end of our republic, because approximately 50 % of the nation apparently believes the same way he does. And nobody seems willing to hold Obama accountable for the poorest performing government in history. I am sure our God does.

Our current political leadership is a mirror of ourselves. It is what we have become. A greedy nation with no respect for the rule of law at the highest office in the land.

And so in my life time I may have seen come to pass the demise of the nation I have held so dear.

Some will say . . . Oh you are being too dramatic. Perhaps the next four years will work things out for the best and in Nov 2016 we can vote in a more constitutionally centered President.

Think about it. Would such a President really change anything? If Mitt Romney had won the election the Senate would have stopped his every move. And we the people hired the Senate as now constituted.

You see our form of government can only flourish in a nation of free men who are interested in remaining free. Men who genuinely believe that we are endowed by our Creator with certain unalienable rights. Men and women who understand this principle and who care. And here's the rub . . . those who understand and care must be in the majority. We are no longer that kind of a nation.

I don't believe that the government of our nation will survive another four years.

A Prophet who lived on the Americas between 600 and 592 BC, said a Church is going to rule the world in these last days.

And that ruling entity is nowhere to be seen . . . at present (See chapter 10).

The "Church" spoken of in chapter 10 could be made up of any world groups or combination of groups, and organizations. This prophet even went so far as to say that everyone in the world *"will belong to one of two churches"*. This world wide membership prophesy by 1st Nephi is also a condition that doesn't exist at present but will most certainly come to past exactly as he prophesied.

The "Church of the devil", discussed in chapter 10, I am sure, presently exists in some form or another. However this eventual "world ruling power" has not yet been made manifest to the world.

Our modern day prophets have not yet revealed when this Church of the Devil will emerge as a world power. They really don't have to. I believe it will become apparent through media sources.

The acceptance by the world of a church shouldn't be surprising to anyone. It is a matter of public record that governments, world wide, have failed man dismally.

Our own government has been judged, by the governed citizens, to be the poorest performing government in memory.

This political situation we find ourselves in today is reminesient of a similar experience the Nephites had about 30 BC. In the Book of Mormon, Helaman 5:2 records *"For as their laws and their governments were established by the voice of the people, and they who chose evil were more numerous than those who chose good, therefore they were ripening for destruction, for the laws had become corrupted"*.

On Jan 17, 2013 I heard a Fox News analyst on the business channel discussing the forth coming "fiscal cliff". He actually said that *"in a year or so their may be no government"*. And all conservative talk show host are convinced that the President and his Democratic allies are trying hard to destroy the "Republican Party" the countries political check and balance party.

In addition on 30 Jan 2013 at 3:22 PM Bret Baier a fox news anchor announced that one of the supreme court justices, Anthony Scalia, during a lecture to a group of lawyers declared: *"the constitution is dead . . . dead . . . dead"*. Meaning that this Heavenly provided document has been so abused and modified that it has lost its original purpose and intent.

The most conspicuous culprit of the loss of good government is the blatant failure of the media to hold government accountable.

I believe that sometime, in the next four years . . . before the November 2016 vote for President, the Church of the Devil will come into power.

What will bring this new world power on to the world scene is anyone's guess.

I suppose that the very aggressive and liberal agenda of this Marxist President, over the months ahead, will be a catalyst to unprecedented despair and anguish among the constitutionalist and religionist of the country. Maybe that will be the "trigger".

A blind man can see that this President and his plans are dividing the country.

Its plain that this divisiveness is causing great consternation among the citizens. And that is an interesting point as one of the tenets of the Karl Marx philosophy of government is to create "division and chaos" in order to gain the advantage over opponents. This Marxist President and his very large staff, and congressional associates have made famous the quote *"all crises are an opportunity"*. And that is exactly what is happening. If a crisis doesn't exist they will create one. Such as a Benghazi, or illegal confiscation of AP reporter records, or illegal behavior by the IRS.

Which by the way ties up the congress in investigations while the white house wages war with the coal industry through onerous regulations issued by executive order.

I anticipate that in the next year or two this deliberate divisiveness on the part of the democrats will achieve "critical mass" and reach the point of open rebellion on the part of more conservative citizens. After all this nation was founded on the principle of revolt against tyranny.

But the most frightening thing our present elected leaders are teaching us by example is . . . no regard for the rule of law.

We, as a nation, of our own free will and choice have departed from Gods "rule of law" and chosen another way and must bear the consequences of our actions.

However we are fortunate that our God is merciful and will bless us and save us from ourselves . . . even by the apocalypse if necessary.

I do not look forward to the next two years. I believe they will be . . . gut wrenching, to say the least, as our elected Marxist President and his political associates, and like minded political base . . . who have obtained through him . . . precedent; and an open door to manipulate, influence, and dismantle, our nation bit by bit. They will think they are securing their wealth and power into perpetuity but they are doing the will of Satan. Our

God will allow this because it is "the will of the people" . . . by with drawing His spirit from this nation as He did with the Pharaoh of Egypt about 1600 BC over the issue of the release from bondage of the Tribes of Israel.

The days ahead are going to be interesting to watch. I am so grateful I have loyalties and deep affections to the Church of Jesus Christ of Latter Day Saints. These feelings, for the church, provide me with great purpose and comfort at the sad prospect of the demise of the nation I have known and loved.

Am I frightened by all of this? By no means. It tells me that the will of the Lord is going forward just as planned.

CHAPTER 14

JOY OF THE FAITHFUL

This chapter is written to introduce another experience that will evolve from the apocalypse and that is the experience of joy. The scriptures tell us *"men are that they might have joy"* (2 Nephi 2:25). To me that sounds very much like the purpose of our existence is to be happy. To experience the joy that comes from a loving Father in Heaven.

The "last days" and "joy" are terms that seem to be completely incompatible. "Last days" is a term that brings images of horror as a righteous God pummels the earth to rid it of evil. The people of the world will be divided into two groups by virtue of the apocalypse. One group will repent and be saved and the other will be destroyed.

However before this "cleansing process" begins, in the world, the Lord will divide His Church into two groups. One group will become offended and join the world and the other will be forced into exile. This last group will have a path of "joy" laid before them.

The scriptures tell us, *"Adam fell that man might be, and men are that they might have joy"* (see 2 Nephi 2:25).

The purpose of our being, since our beginning as a corporeal intelligence . . . a spirit, . . . and continuing as a mortal, has been that of obtaining joy.

From Job 38:4-7, we read, *"Where wast thou when I laid the foundations of the earth? Declare if thou hast understanding. Who hath laid the measure thereof, if thou knowest? Or who hath stretched the line upon it? Whereupon are the foundations thereof fastened? Or who hath laid the corner stone thereof; When the morning stars sang together, and all the sons of God shouted for joy".*

This is a very telling scripture, and speaks to a time when all the spirit children of God who were assigned to this earth *"shouted for joy"*, at the prospect of one day coming to this earth . . . an earth that, at that time, had not yet been constructed.

This jubilant shout occurred at a time when the *"corner stone was laid"*, for the construction of the earth, and at the laying of the corner stone the *"morning stars"* . . . the spirit off spring of God (you and I . . . dear reader), *"shouted for joy"*.

As any builder knows the laying of the corner stone is one of the first and vital steps to building a structure and having it turn out to be true and properly aligned. The foundation of a structure . . . aligns to the corner stone.

The morning stars shouted for joy, at the laying of the corner stone, before the foundations of this earth were laid.

Our Prophets estimate that the organized earth is millions of years old (see note 3). Obviously we have been spirit children of our Heavenly Father for a very long time. And on this glorious occasion we were excited and happy at the prospect of progressing through a mortal experience on a new earth and to eventually become immortal like our divine parents.

I have always wondered what we did in our 1st estate, which apparently was a very long, long time. Oh I understand about the council in Heaven and Satan's bid to be the executor of the plan of salvation and his subsequent rejection by the Father . . . and the ensuing war in heaven (See Revelation 12:7-9). I know that those in mortality were on the right side of this conflict, in the 1st estate. But what else did I do?

And then I found the answer to my question.

Some years ago at a stake Conference in the Puyallup, Washington Stake we had a general authority visitor by the name of Elder Glenn L Pace. In his address to the adult session Saturday evening, as near as I can recall, he spoke to the theme, something like, "Who are you"? This message turned out to be a life changing experience for me. And I expect not just for me alone but for the rest of the congregation as well. Because when time came to close the meeting the spirit was so strong there was not a sound to be heard in the packed congregation. And Elder Pace, sensing our feelings, said something to the effect . . . "I feel that you would like me to continue" . . . and he did, for another 20 minutes.

The thought I came way from that meeting with . . . was that in the pre-existence I had a role in the creation of this earth. I had no idea what kind of a role or in what capacity, but I definitely felt I was involved. In fact I feel that I have been associated with this earth since the time of its spiritual creation. And if I am faithful I will be privileged to continue to be associated with this earth . . . that obeys the measure of her creation.

Early, in my church career I was somewhat frustrated by the parable of the "Talents" found in Mathew 25:14-30. Because I wondered "what talent did the Lord give me, during my pre-existent life, that He expected me to *"add upon"* in mortality? And it seemed logical to me that whatever talent I had I used and developed in the spirit world.

But what talent did I have? I pondered on this subject and prayed about it but . . . nothing. And it was apparent to me, from this scripture in Matthew, that proper use of ones talent is necessary to succeed in mortality. And then I had an experience that answered that question unequivocally.

Several years after the Stake conference, with Elder Pace, a part of our Stake was involved in flooding from a river that flowed over its banks. Members of the Stake rushed to help a flooded mobile home park. While standing next to me on a knoll over looking the park the 1ˢᵗ counselor in the Stake Presidency, commented to me that he "didn't know where to begin" . . . as he surveyed the damage, and lingering pools of water and mud.

At the time I was in the High Council and one of my assignments, over stake welfare, brought me to this sad sight.

And in response to his comment I said. *"Oh President that is easy. Just divide our crew into three teams and send them down these three major roads and interview the people and ascertain their needs. Some residence have flood insurance and don't want things disturbed until the insurance companies have seen the extent of the damage. While others have no flood insurance and will need help to salvage what they can".*

Where upon the President turned to me and said . . . "you are a natural logistician".

That was it. Everything in me said this is your talent and you have just learned it from a humble Priesthood servant of the Lord. I received a spiritual confirmation that his observation was correct.

I now believe that in the pre-existence I worked on this earth, both in its spiritual and temporal creation, in the capacity of a logistician.

And as I thought about this "talent" I realized that in one way or another I have used this skill all my life. For 35 years I was a buyer for a large aircraft and defense systems manufacture and it was my job to support a manufacturing line in order to meet schedules and deliveries to military customers. I was comfortable in this work . . . it seemed natural.

I am confident that every child of our Heavenly Father has some unique talent that was part of their calling and duty in their 1st estate. And that as we mature in the gospel these gifts become manifest and provide experiences that are "comfortable and familiar" to us, and give us a measure of joy.

Knowing who we really are, can be a source of great strength and purpose to us in this mortal experience.

Obviously each and every mortal was successful enough in the 1st estate to come to earth in order to be *"added upon"*. However we are only here for a very short time. So knowing *"who you really are"* can be a great motivational blessing to each of us.

Even though mortality is a short time it is a vastly important time. Our entire future eternity, as an immortal being, depends on this very short time in mortality. And it's very obvious that those of our Heavenly Fathers children who succeed in this second estate will experience joy. And those who are not successful will not. Whether we succeed in this estate or not our next estate will be as an immortal.

It seems to me that joy is an experience associated with accomplishment. When I graduated from school I felt some joy but mostly relief. When I have been privileged to baptize someone I helped bring to the waters of baptism . . . my joy is great and even accompanied with tears of joy. It happens again when I go to the Temple with that same someone a year later.

I have learned that all inspiration from the spirit, even . . . chastisement, is accompanied with feelings of joy and instruction.

From our beginning in the spirit world we have struggled and worked for success . . . probably measured in terms of parental approval. Such as that great council in Heaven referred to above, in Job 38:4-7. That was graduation day for most of us and in our exuberance we shouted for joy.

I would imagine that over eons of time, in our first estate, we have sought for the circumstances and conditions that elicited approval from our loving immortal parents. These are learned conditions that carry over into mortality. However there are differing degrees of joy. In the presence of God we can experience what the scriptures refer to as a "fullness of joy", and then only as a resurrected and immortal being.

I can only imagine that a "fullness of joy", is associated with the privileges of godhood such as the authority and the power to create, the *"continuation of the seed"*, eternal association with loved ones, and after teaching, observation and experience, . . . the blessing of omnipotence (see D/C 132:19-20).

So here we are today, in the world of man, and with no recollection of our long and glorious past.

Our Prophets tell us we were held back to come forth in this, the "dispensation of the fullness of times", because of our *"exceeding great faith in the first place"* (see Alma 13:1-11).

Our time in mortality was carefully planned and prepared for. Nothing so significant as the birth of a child is by chance.

We are privileged to live in the most interesting and significant dispensation of time.

A dispensation when the true church was restored and the Lords library, of revelation covering many millennia, is available to us. We also live at a time when temples are beginning to fill the earth and a covenant people are once again found on the earth.

However as righteousness makes progress Satan is presently permitted, to likewise, increase effort . . . for the souls of man.

So while there is great righteousness on the earth, today, there is also great evil.

In the year 2013 the faithful saints find themselves in a church with the largest membership ever experienced, in fact the LDS Church is the fourth largest Christian Church in the world and, at present, has an unprecedented 141 operating temples world wide. However Satan is also having great success in the world, as we know, and we now live in a world with unprecedented evil.

I can only guess at the level of wickedness in the plains cities of Sodom and Gomorrah that so disgusted the Lord that he rained fire from heaven on these two cities and destroyed them.

However I suspect that our own societies today are, in all probability, every bit as evil and decadent as Sodom and Gomorrah and that on a global scale.

What possible joy can the saints elicit from this unhappy news? The answer to that interrogative is . . . every bit of joy and in every way. How so?

Our general authorities constantly remind us that this life is but a phase in our eternal journey.

That the . . . thinking, smiling, vibrant personality that you are . . . , is indestructible.

And all saints have entered into the Abrahamic covenant of "Salvation" through the waters of baptism. Further more we know that our Heavenly Father is omnipotent. Nothing happens in our world that doesn't lend itself to His purposes. We are . . . , or should be, . . . the happiest people on earth.

The scriptures tell us, unequivocally, that we are the saints of the last days. And as such we will have a role in the winding down scenes of our present telestial world and the beginning of the terrestrial world to follow. Oh what joy and privilege to serve, uplift, and enlighten that will be.

The day is not far off, when the Lord will stand on this earth. First in Adam-Ondi-Amen, and then in His triumphant return to earth. These are events that every prophet and peoples in every millennium have looked forward to and sang about.

During the millennium, I believe that, one of our terrestrial assignments, will be to establish our family links from Adam to the newest born in the New Jerusalem. And we won't be alone. We will have all of those who will come forth in the morning and the afternoon of the 1st resurrection. We will meet and work with souls we have taken to the temple in our present day world. And these people, who have the same interest and training as we do in genealogy work, will have just come from a close association with theirs and our kindred dead in the spirit world. They will have all family names and dates we need to complete our lines. And we will be working shoulder to shoulder with our "kindred dead".

Of all the people on this earth we should be the happiest and filled with quiet confidence and joy even as frightening world scenes unfold. We have been prepared for this day . . . this is our time on earth.

I believe we have been prepared for the dramatic events that are explained in chapters 6 and 7.

Events and circumstances that will change our lives. Our experiences will be no more dramatic than those of our pioneer ancestors who struggled across the plains in the middle of winter . . . driven by their faith who . . . *"no toil or labor feared, but with joy wend your way"*. They fled the evil of the world for the harsh freedom of the wilderness, and the eventual joy in the "tops of the hills" . . . of Zion.

We will do the same for Zion and "The New Jerusalem".

We will have been taken out of the most wicked world of any dispensation of time. Its true we will no longer have the luxuries we once enjoyed, in fact we won't own anything, and we will be considered outlaws, but that doesn't seem important.

When the saints agree to live the law of consecration they agree to live a celestial law, and will reap the blessings associated with that law.

I believe that the people who accept the law of consecration will be as varied as we are now in our congregations. Those who choose to exodus will consist of families, . . . and maybe not all of a family. There will also be single adults, young single adults, and lots of youth and children.

I believe that exile societies, for the saints, will be set-up in small well organized and communal groups . . . and will be as fulfilling as circumstances may permit. I would guess schools, for children, would be established and all religious meetings of course. Also the saints have always loved music to lift spirits and extend encouragement. Young single adults, and single adults, may date and their may even be marriages in these exile societies.

In exile the saints will be busy, learning and teaching how to survive in a communal, frontier-like, environment. Organizing and maintaining supplies, and housing. In effect setting up a functioning society, . . . one that will accomplish the will of the Lord.

History has taught that the saints when forced into rustic circumstances have always been inclined to make the best of it and establish societal behavior that is both enriching and uplifting.

Priesthood will be sent on assignments, into the world, to save the honest in heart and such other assignments as the Lord decrees. These elect saints will be the Lords missionaries, and ministers to the world and they will be located in every nation where the church is located today.

I believe that the elect must remain in the world, in the nation they now reside in, and contend with the "Beast" for 3.5 years. The "Beast" is to the Last Days Saints as the Jews and the Romans were to the Meridian-of days-Saints.

During this exile the elect will become so conversant with the Holy Ghost that to be without him would make one feel lonely and empty . . . almost forsaken.

The war with the "Beast" will be one sided. The saints will have no stomach for killing or crippling any mortal. Best just to avoid them.

Lets summarize the joy of the "Elect", in the path that lies before them:

* ★ The decision to live the law of consecration will be a most solemn, personal and private occasion. However once the decision is made and confirmed by the signing *"of an oath and covenant"*, the mantle of this celestial law

will pass upon the faithful with feelings of confidence and completeness never before experienced. Because such a law has never been part of our lives. Once the value of properties *"are laid at the feet of the Apostles"* the lives of the faithful will have entered into feelings of commitment, never before experienced. This level of commitment is calming, and peaceful and is the foundation of joy as one moves closer to the Lord.

★ Having laid the foundation the faithful are now ready to *"Go where you want me to go dear Lord",* and will exodus the world of man to locations the Priesthood will have pre-arranged. Now the faithful are co-mingled with only the elect.

The spirit of the Lord will begin to be felt as unrestrained in their lives. They will begin, almost immediately to feel very positive, stronger, more mentally alert. They will have feelings of eagerness to succeed and achieve. They will experience all the noble feelings that come from the Holy Ghost. Church meetings, even in rustic settings, will be unprecedented in spiritual manifestations. Joy and wonderment will be almost daily fare for the "Elect". They will truly feel that they are in the world but . . . not part of it.

★ The war with the "Beast" will be an interesting experience. The "Beast" hasn't the slightest possibility of success. Every assignment to the "Elect", by the Priesthood will be faithfully accomplished. The Holy Ghost who is the master of all things will be the companion on every venture, by the saints, to fulfill assignments in the world of man. Not withstanding the "war", life in exile for the saints will be full and happy. Just like the Saints of the Meridian of time who were in self imposed exile for "fear of the Jews", who also knew the joy of living the law of consecration, for they too "*had all things in common*".

★ The war with the "Beast" is decreed to last 3.5 years. At the end of that time the saints will walk about in the world of man under the divine protection of the Lord. But the Lord doesn't want his saints co-mingling with the world of man so He will call them to another exodus . . . to Jackson County, Missouri which will have been prepared for the faithful. The exodus to Missouri will be a very happy event for the saints. In Missouri they will be assigned their inheritance by the Presiding Bishopric (see D/C 85) and will be amazed at the general feelings of joy and peace. Here they will meet dear friends and family who they were separated from, and will fall on their necks with tears of joy and love.

Life in Zion will be busy. There is so much to do. Preparation needs to made for:

★ The influx of souls hastening to escape the days of "tribulation and desolation".

★ And for the gathering of the Lamanites who are to be taught the gospel.

★ And for the building of a magnificent temple with a gate for each of the tribes of Israel.

★ And the "Brethren" are planning for a great Priesthood meeting to be held, not to far away, in "Adam-Ondi-Amen".

★ And we know from the teachings of the Prophets that the ten tribes will be joining us soon from the North.

★ And also the return to earth of the City of Enoch. And the joy associated with that momentous event.

★ But the greatest of all blessings, one can imagine, is the Second Coming of the Lord and His residence on this earth.

Oh the wonder of it all, the magnificence, the grandeur, the inspiration, one can scarce take it in, and yet this is the destiny for the faithful that begins . . . *"at a time yet to be revealed".*

Those of the tribe of Ephraim will have responsibility to plan, prepare and execute all things, beginning with the Law of consecration to the establishment of New Jerusalem, and the providing of blessings upon the Lamanites, the tribes from the North and the return of the city of Enoch. In fact preparing all things for the Second Coming, in the New Jerusalem, will be the responsibility of those of the tribe of Ephraim of the House of Israel.

It gives me . . . pause . . . just to consider how great is the Priesthood that has been assigned to this earth in these last days, among all the infinite creations of the Lord.

Prophets have seen the events, that I have lightly touched upon here, through the millennia of time. These are joyous events that have been prophetically reported to buoy the heart and strengthen the resolve of true worshippers since time began. And here we are, the saints of latter days, held back to come forth in the very hour when these marvelous events are to come to pass as prophesied.

Not only are we to witness these things but we have the privilege to be participants. This is the joy of the faithful in these last days.

But let us be very clear about one thing . . . the path to the joy *"that lies before us"* is the path of the *"hard choice".* This will be the choice to live the Law of Consecration *"at a time yet to be revealed"*. A choice to live a celestial law with the absolute guarantee of persecution for 3.5 years . . . and the beginning of joy.

Note 3: Modern scientists through the science of carbon dating have concluded that the earth is 4.5 billion years old. However, I believe that this dating applies to particulate matter and not too organized matter. Eric Skousen in his book "Earth in the Beginning", (a recommended reading) on pages 155-159, cites quotes from many church leaders and well known church writers who have made statements to the effect that the modern _organized earth_ is millions of years old. These include quotes from Brigham Young, Orson Pratt, John Taylor, John A Widtsoe, BH Roberts, James E Talmage, David O McKay, and others. I think it is safe to conclude that the spirit children of God are, at least, millions of years old. However, as I understand the timing of our earth, "modern mortal Man", starting with Adam down through the ages to you and I; has been on this earth, just 6,012 years, and a little bit, as of the time of this writing.

CHAPTER 15

SUMMARY

The purpose of these "Apocalyptic writings" is to convey a warning. And the message is clear . . . repent and prepare your selves to meet our God.

The foregoing description of events that will occur before the Lord comes, is preparatory to the earth becoming a terrestrial world. It will continue as a terrestrial world for one-thousand years, during the period known as the Millennium.

Only those souls who qualify for a terrestrial world will be protected from much of the horror described in the foregoing chapters.

All souls who live a telestial law, and who do not repent, will not survive the cleansing.

People who have rejected the missionaries of the LDS Church but who are "honorable men and women of the world", or those who have "no law", such as aborigines or the mentally deficient are in the final judgment entitled to a terrestrial degree of glory (see D/C 76:71-79).

All who could qualify for the terrestrial kingdom because of the law they live in mortality, will be entitled to continue with the earth as it dons its terrestrial and paradisiacal splendor.

It appears that the <u>minimal standard</u> of acceptance to be spared destruction during the apocalypse is what the scriptures refer to as an "honorable man". A person may ask? What standard does one have to meet to be considered an honorable man or woman? *"These are they who are honorable man of the earth, who were blinded by the craftiness of men"* (D/C 76:75).

My opinion of an "honorable man or woman" is one who respects our Heavenly Father, and is not given to profanity, or excessive drink or the use of habituating drugs. Is morally chaste. Does not cheat their fellowman, and has a good sense of right and wrong. They love their family, and see that their children get a good education, and are raised to show respect for the rights and properties of others. Such a person does not engage in gossip, and is not a liar. They respect the rule of law. They honor the principle of marriage as set forth by Heavenly Father.

I have just described the neighbors of many latter-day-saints who have rejected the missionary efforts of the LDS Church.

Will they experience fear, despair and hopelessness during the apocalypse?

Most definitely! It is those feelings that will motivate them to "turn their hearts toward Heaven".

I personally believe that such individuals regardless of religious affiliation will be filtered out of our wicked society, by the events of the apocalypse, and be spared to live, on this earth, during the millennial reign of the Lord.

From my study of these "Last Days" scriptures I have learned that there will be several migrations from the world to a place of security and protection . . . Jackson County, Missouri.

The first is the gathering of the elect.

The second group will be those who have been motivated by the frightening and horrible events of the last days. Most probably *"honorable men and women of the world"*, who recognize that something is terribly wrong, in their world, and look for a safe haven. History will have caught up with these souls and they will know the LDS Church was right. They will repent and be permitted to flee to Zion.

A third group will be those *"who refuse to take up the sword against his neighbor who will flee to Zion for safety"* See D/C 45:68). These people have a "live and let Live", philosophy of life. They "wink" at the sins of their neighbors, but draw the line at the thought of taking the life of any of their fellow man.

Apparently the threat of universal war will send many peoples of the world scurrying to Zion for safety. Hate will be so pervasive among the wicked of the world that they will take up weapons against one another. Obviously those of the wicked who have no desire to engage in warfare will certainly be more righteous, than those who are thoroughly in Satan's power, and they will flee to Zion for safety.

A fourth group will be those who are of the blood of Israel, whether by blood or adoption, (baptism into the Church) who have not been valiant in the work of the Lord, who will be given one more chance to repent. If they do so the Lord will save them. They too will be taught by the conclusive truth of "history". History is a recognition of the facts . . . after the facts have occurred.

I believe this group will also include the "Lamanites", who are to be taught the gospel.

Clearly the Lord is making every effort to fulfill His covenant to Israel the Patriarch (See 3rd Nephi 21:20-23).

I believe that this fourth group is the last and final separation of the principled from the unprincipled.

The Lord in D/C 45:69, declared, *"And there shall be gathered unto it (Zion) out of every nation under heaven; and it shall be the only people that shall not be at war one with another"*.

It would appear from these scriptures that the events of the last days are refiners and purifiers of the hearts of men. At least those men who have the presence of mind to recognize history when it occurs.

In 2 Nephi 30:10, the Lord declared *"For the time speedily cometh that the Lord God shall cause a great division among the people, and the wicked will he destroy; and he will spare his people, yea, even if it so be that he must destroy the wicked by fire"*. The term "the people" has reference to the people of the "world", as opposed to "his people" meaning the people of His church.

I submit that the great division that will occur among "the people" will happen as a result of the divisiveness of the Obama administration. The Obama Presidency marks the beginning of the events of the last days, hence "The Apocalypse has begun".

The events following the public acceptance of the world wide church, will be the purging of the LDS Church, starting with the *"Law of Consecration"* This will be the day of the *"hard choice"*, for the latter-day-saints.

One may ask, why wouldn't the wicked of the world go up to war against the saints when they are congregated in the New Jerusalem, or Zion? Surly the implements of war at the disposal of the people of the world could reduce Zion to a cinder.

Again in D/C 45:70 the Lord revealed, *"And it shall be said among the wicked: Let us not go up to battle against Zion, for the inhabitants of Zion are a terrible people; wherefore we cannot stand"*.

Clearly the Lord will put fear in the hearts of the wicked of the world as it pertains to warfare with the Lords "elect", and the "gathered". Such fear is not without good reason. It is prompted by the Holy Ghost and is wisely heeded. Our God who can change water to wine by taking thought (see John 2: 1-11) and feed 5000 souls with 5 loves of bread and several fishes . . . through faith in prayer . . . and still collect 12 baskets of fragments, from the feeding, is not one to be trifled with (see Matthew 14: 17-21). Or consider the mighty power of this omnipotent God, to whom the basic elements of all matter are obedient, who walks on water, and commands the mighty winds and raging sea . . . . *"peace . . . be still"*. (see Matt 14:24-33, and Mark 4:37-41).

The weapons of man are puny compared to the power the Lord can muster. As we will all learn!

And so it seems that those who will not succumb to the evil influence of Satan will be driven out of the world into the arms of the "elect" in Zion. These will also participate in the building up of the New Jerusalem.

They may or may not join the Church. Brigham Young in his journal of discourses, in speaking of Zion, said; *"I presume there will be as many different sects and parties then as are now. Will the Jews and the gentiles be obliged to belong to the Church? No! Not by any means."* (Journal of Discourses vol. Xl., page 275).

However Satan will be bound because terrestrial souls are not vulnerable to his enticing. They have established and maintained disciplines in their lives that are more righteous. They are

God fearing people who understand the value of divine and wholesome law in their lives. Law that is practical and leads to a smooth and orderly life. They are "honorable men and women" and do not listen to Satan and he will be ignored. These people will live in a Terrestrial environment, a time, when "*the gospel of the Lord Jesus Christ will cover the earth like a flood*".

In conclusion I want to submit another thought relative to the physical appearance of the saints and those who qualify to remain on this earth as it progresses into the millennium. I believe that in general appearance, once we have reached the age of mid-thirties, we will look like the Lord . . . as it relates to the appearance of age. We will look thirty-ish even though we will age chronologically. Not only well we look younger but I believe we will have the strength and vitality one would associate with that approximate age. To my thinking this is only logical. All those who come forth in the morning and afternoon of the first resurrection will look the same age as the Lord who was crucified at age 33 and resurrected himself 3 days later(see KJV Bible, chronology, page 644). And I like to think that those who remain mortal and survive the "Restoration" will look the same age as the resurrected Lord and the many, many resurrected people who will come forth in the morning and the afternoon of the 1ˢᵗ resurrection.

Our God is marvelous beyond imagination. Not only will He manage all the events of the last days, in accordance with the schedule He has revealed, but He will provide opportunity for unprecedented joy to those who have proven faithful in all things . . . to the very end.

Thought and language fail in consideration of the blessings and privileges the Lord will make available to the faithful of the House of Israel. The Prophets throughout the millennia of time have not been able to express the joy that will come to the "Elect" in this last half-hour of "Mother Earth's" telestial estate, and restoration and renewal to her terrestrial estate. Joy that, I sense, *"surpasses all understanding"*.